Madras, Chenna
Conversations ۱ ۔۔۔ ۔۱۔y

Born in 1967 in Madras, Tulsi Badrinath has a Bachelor's degree in English Literature from Stella Maris College and an MBA from Ohio University, Athens. After four long, dreary years in a multinational bank, Tulsi quit her job to pursue her passion for writing and dance.

Her birthplace is also her chosen home. The city has always been central to Tulsi's work – *Madras, Chennai and the Self: Conversations with the City* is her fourth book on the subject, adding substantially to the Madras body of work that includes two novels, *Meeting Lives* and *Man of A Thousand Chances*, both longlisted for the Man Asian Literary Prize, and one of narrative non-fiction, *Master of Arts, A Life in Dance*.

Her poems, articles, reviews and short stories have appeared in *India Today, The Week, The Hindu, New Indian Express, Deccan Herald* and *Namaste* among others.

Tulsi was trained in Bharatanatyam from the age of eight by the Dhananjayans, and has performed solo widely, in India and abroad.

Praise for *Madras, Chennai and the Self:*
Conversations with the City

'A narrative of the city in which the life-force of the subject is always present, as is the physical fragment of the city they occupy along with the author herself – perceptive, observant, sympathetic and even wistful. Those who love Madras and Chennai owe Tulsi special thanks for such a vivid and eloquent celebration of that spirit'
– *The Indian Express*

'This book is not a conventional book about Chennai. It is an exploration of the city through the experience of 12 individuals drawn from different walks of life. While there is some familiarity when one reads the book, the author springs many surprises'
– *The Statesman*

'Badrinath's book manages to be different by focusing on people, their lives and their world views, and consequently their experience of the city – in sharp focus or soft. The seamless way in which information about the city, its landmarks – many unheralded, even unknown – is presented is appealing because it is unselfconscious and the writing clean and upfront'
– *The Hindu Business Line*

'For people who have travelled to many places and made the city their abode, this book will surely strike a chord, as one will surely find several similar experiences, like the ones narrated by Tulsi'
– *The New Indian Express*

'Happily, Tulsi Badrinath's *Madras, Chennai and the Self: Conversations with the City* … attempts a creative and entirely new path in profiling the metropolis'
– *The Hindu Literary Review*

'A fresh and unconventional perspective. An arresting read'
– *Hindustan Times*

Madras, Chennai and the Self
Conversations with the City

For Mary,
Thank you for taking
so much trouble over me!
Warmly,
Tulsi
Liverpool '16

Tulsi Badrinath

PAN

First published in India 2015 by Pan
an imprint of Pan Macmillan India,
a division of Macmillan Publishers India Limited
Pan Macmillan India,
707, Kailash Building 26, K.G. Marg, New Delhi – 110 001
www.panmacmillan.co.in

Pan Macmillan, 20 New Wharf Road, London N1 9RR
Basingstoke and Oxford
Associated companies throughout the world
www.panmacmillan.com

ISBN 978-93-82616-23-8
Copyright © Tulsi Badrinath 2015

Typeset by Malhotra Designer and Printers
Printed and bound in India by
Replika Press Pvt. Ltd.

Dedicated to the memory of

M Krishnan and Indumati Krishnan

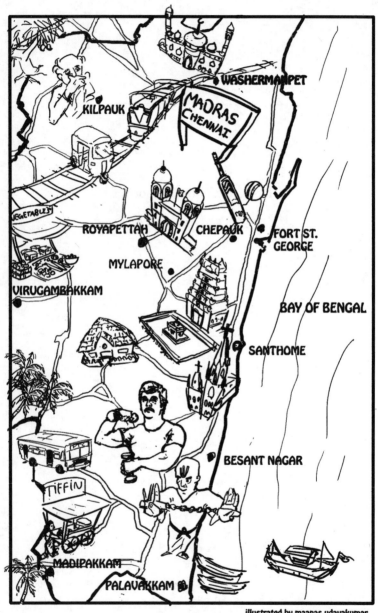

WASHERMANPET

KILPAUK

MADRAS
CHENNAI

VEGETABLES

ROYAPETTAH   CHEPAUK   FORT ST. GEORGE

MYLAPORE

VIRUGAMBAKKAM

BAY OF BENGAL

SANTHOME

TIFFIN

BESANT NAGAR

MADIPAKKAM

PALAVAKKAM

illustrated by maanas udayakumar
map not to scale

Contents

With whose love are you smitten?

With whose love are you smitten,
O sea?
For among the woods of the shore
where like the small-headed goats
from the Pooli land,
seagulls thronged and fished,
your waves kept lashing
against the screw pines
bearing white blossoms
and even in the dead of the night
I hear your voice.

(what the girl said)

— Neidal
Ammuvanar
Kurunthokai 163

Introduction

One of my earliest memories of Madras is of oil lamps radiant in the dusk, just outside the compound of our house.

There, on the other side of the hedge, visible during the day and worshipped at night, were several anthills, long cones of mud with snake burrows underground. In the evenings, passers-by lit oil lamps, poured milk and left eggs at the shrine of the snake gods. Warm flames flickered at dusk, rendering alive the primordial mounds adorned with red *kumkum* and red hibiscus flowers. When it turned dark, the golden light wavered in the wind, conical shadows turned taller and there was a palpable sense of the mystic.

I never saw the snakes.

The anthills had sprung up recently, as also the shrine, similar to others scattered throughout the city at the root of old trees in groves, or those by the road. At some point, my father, irked by the increasingly large, noisy gatherings just outside our gate and the imminent possibility that they would encroach on public land and build a permanent shrine, or perhaps worried that there were indeed snakes so close to our home, ordered the hillocks to be razed. No one protested. The holes were filled up, and that evening there was only absence, the darkness, and thwarted, puzzled wayfarers who carried their offerings home.

This deep-rooted memory carries within it the sense of something enduring, beyond all time – dusk, the gesture of setting a wick alight, the basic sustenance from soil, veneration of forces larger than oneself, the juncture of night and day. Each passing year added layer upon layer of other similar memories, a vertical connection between sky and earth as it were. In this city, there is a strong connection between the seasons and customs, between man and nature, linking the 'new' of the past to the 'old' of the present.

As far back as perhaps the second century BCE, the ancient Tamils had invoked the seashore and coastal areas as part of a five-fold landscape that was as much emotional as it was geographical. Hugged by the Bay of Bengal along its shore, where fisherfolk ruled the waves, the city-that-was-yet-to-be fell into the *neidal* category of classical Sangam literature, one that described the pining of a lover. The natural location and the human condition, one signifying the other, were intertwined in that central experience, love, in all its rich variety.

I grew to understand that ancient fabric such as this, of poetry and emotions, of simple faith and undying mores, supports the more obvious cement-and-steel manifestations of this modern metropolis, recently named the best Indian city to live in by *India Today*.

The wide Edward Elliots Road, near the nursing home where I was born, led straight onto the open vista of blue sky, sand and the endless waters of the Bay of Bengal. It was in these nautical miles that a particular ship anchored in 1639, from which its passengers had to take a smaller boat to reach the shore.

When Francis Day stepped on a sandy strip of land five kilometres in length and two kilometres in width on the Coromandel Coast nearly four centuries ago, it was not only an exploratory step on behalf of a trading company but a giant stride into the future of imperial Britain.

All that the East India Company needed was a warehouse for their trading activities, a place where they could source an uninterrupted supply of 'painted cloth' or chintz for sale in

Britain. Demarcated on two sides by rivers and on the east by the sea, the natural features of this 'no man's land' must have appealed to Day, even though for years to come, crossing the unruly sea between ship and land would be a feat in itself.

At that potent moment on 27 August 1639 when the village of Madraspatnam was given to the Company by Damarla Venkatappa Nayak and his brother Ayyappa, for a period of two years, along with the right to build a fort, issue coins and govern the area, Francis Day and his boss Andrew Cogan could not have foreseen the far-reaching consequences this simple act would have.

They started work on a fort in February 1640, and a rudimentary Fort House, all of one hundred yards square, was completed by April 23, which happened to be St. George's Day.

The outer ramparts of the Fort enclosed the 'White Town' of about seventy houses. This, then, was the extent of Madras and the only big structure on the skyline.

In the area Chennapatnam, to the north of the Fort and outside its walls, lived some 300 families of weavers and craftsmen. They had been settled there, in the 'Black Town', by *dubash* and interpreter Beri Thimappa, considered one of the founders of the city because he helped negotiate the grant of land. Madraspatnam and Chennapatnam, together representing the city, were referred to as Chennai in the local speech, or even more simply as Patnam by those who lived in the villages and smaller towns radiating far inland.

Slowly, the number of British and Portuguese living in the Fort grew. And in time, more villages, such as Triplicane, were added to the first one. Mylapore – land of the peacock's cry – a few kilometres away from Fort St. George, had been considered a sacred place as far back perhaps as the first century BCE, and when it was included in the growing city of

Madras, it also became one of its oldest localities. All these villages lay outside the boundary of the Fort, and as the city of Madras grew to its present size, so did the number of villages included within its greater area, while the Fort itself did not grow substantially past its outer perimeter of about hund- red acres.

Today, the Fort lies so well ensconced within the city that it is hard to imagine the days when the Fort and 'Madras' were geographically congruent.

When my parents took me, their newborn, home it was to San Thome, another locality that had a history far older than the Fort.

Long before Francis Day, other travellers and merchants had taken the sea route and come to the shores of the Coromandel, seeking its wealth. Trade with the Romans can be traced back to the first century CE. That trade continued with the Greeks, the Phoenicians and later the Arabs. It expanded when the Chola empire which was at its height between the ninth and eleventh centuries swept across the seas to secure the Maldives, Sri Lanka and parts of Southeast Asia including present day Cambodia.

The Dutch, the Danish and the French had all interacted with the people who lived in the larger area inland surrounding Madras on three sides. San Thome, which too lay on the coast but south of the Fort, had been occupied by the Portuguese since the early fifteen hundreds.

San Thome is dominated by the spire of the Saint Thomas Basilica, where the relics of the apostle of Christ are buried. We lived about two kilometres away in a flat in the Foreshore Estate, aptly named, for it was very close to the shore and the fishermen's community, those original and eternal inhabitants of Madras. From here, one of our neighbours – Benazir's brother, as I knew him – Nasser Hussain, would travel far to captain England's cricket team.

Later, we moved south of the city – where it was newly expanding in the sixties – south of the river Adyar, to Shastri Nagar where my parents built a house. And it is in this area, again close to the sea, that I have spent most of my life, registering the many changes.

Madras and Chennai came into existence almost simultaneously in 1639, as two contiguous areas. While Madras went on to lend its name to the larger southern peninsula or Madras Presidency, it also absorbed Chennai into its fold as it grew. Debate over the origins of the words Madras and Chennai continues long after the Tamil Nadu government's decision in 1996 to officially change the capital city's name.

In the past ten years especially, there has been rapid change of the sort that leads people to distinguish hip 'Chennai' from boring 'Madras'. So while they were twin names of a settlement, each name has come to represent different qualities depending on the period in question. This fact interests me greatly, for it is not as though there are two different populations inhabiting these two mythical spaces. Everyone lives in this one geographical space.

The city is known to be traditional and modern at the same time. In this somewhat simplistic construct, traditional alludes to the customs and largely conservative values followed for centuries while modern refers to the present, with all its amenities, and the changes in lifestyle wrought by the necessities of living in a metropolis. Some would ascribe the traditional way of life to 'Madras' and the modern novelties to 'Chennai'. But when one looks at history, it is clear that the birth of Madras itself was the 'modern', relative to the present of 1639, in the lives of the people who lived in its contiguous geographical areas such as Mylapore, Triplicane and San Thome.

The city's inhabitants thus have had long practice assimilating change even while adhering to the customs of their village localities. Wherever there is a gap between the way of life implied by certain traditions and the pressures of a modern city, most natives seem to deftly straddle the divide.

While Madras had a headstart of almost fifty years over Calcutta in terms of its pre-eminence in the East India Company's affairs, gradually Calcutta became the centre of its expanding ambitions in the Indian subcontinent. In 1772, Calcutta became the capital of British India and Madras was left to grow at its own pace.

After Independence, various parts of Madras Presidency were allocated to other states, and Madras became the capital of the new state of Tamil Nadu. Today at Fort St. George, the tallest flagmast in the country triumphantly bears the Indian flag, a happy ending that took 300-odd years to achieve.

Its proximity to the sea and a port has meant that travellers from other countries still come here to do business, and with its specialization in car, motorbike, and auto-parts manufacture, it is known as the 'Detroit of India'. A strong government enabled infrastructure for manufacturing has brought many world class companies such as Hyundai, Nokia and Caterpillar to Chennai, while Ford even has its own dedicated car-parking area at the Chennai Port. The quality of advanced medical care offered by its doctors attracts patients from all countries. In December, art lovers arrive to participate in the famous 'season' when over 2000 performances of classical music and dance take place across the city. And through the year, connoisseurs visit the Government Museum, drawn by the world's finest collection of Chola bronzes.

The sea brings dangers as well, such as in 1914 when the German warship Emden, lurked in its waters and bombarded Madras, making it the only Indian city to be attacked during World War I, and ten years ago, in 2004, when the tsunami wreaked havoc.

In 2014, Chennai celebrated its 375th birthday. When asked to write a book on the city, it seemed to me that in order to do that, to actually convey the flavour of life here, I had to write about its people, and the spaces they inhabit. How do people negotiate change? How do they incorporate the new, the different or more importantly the modern notion of individuality into a traditional way of thinking? Through their experiences, perhaps I might learn if there is an immutable core to the city that gives it the strength to accept change, or whether it is ever-evolving.

In a way, I had already described some of the city's characteristics in my novels. If it was the palpable sense of the spiritual in *Meeting Lives*, it was about water shortage, traffic jams, and a strong belief in fate in *Man of A Thousand Chances*. In *Master of Arts*, I had written about my journey in the world of Bharatanatyam, an integral part of the city's culture. But now I had the chance to step out of the zone of imagination and the familiar, to meet strangers and expand my own perspective.

In deciding on whom to interview, I chose people who live in different parts of the city, though I suspect I have ended up being partial to the area south of Adyar where I live. More importantly, I sought those who in some way brought out an aspect of the city. It is an eclectic choice, for a book this length cannot be comprehensive.

Central to the theme of inner spaces, drawing on my memories, is Perunkulam House in Mylapore, the home of the late M Krishnan – the great photographer and wildlife expert, and his wife, Indumati Krishnan.

The Prince of Arcot, K Seshadri and Saravana Sakthivale talk about their experience of tradition and changes wrought by time. Both P Sivakami and Sarathbabu Elumalai exemplify people's faith in education as a means to improving one's circumstances, and both have plunged into politics – that other route to bringing about change. V Ramnarayan's reminiscences trace just how the Englishman's game, cricket, became 'tradition' in Madras, and Dr Uma Ram has daily experience of the clash of superstition with science. 'Chiyaan' Vikram proves that in this city, actors are heroes in true life as well and Kiruba Shankar reveals the reach of cyber space, across all boundaries. Beatrix D'Souza and A Faizur Rahman talk about the spiritual element in the city, of the way it nurtures different faiths. A thread of unmistakable pride in the city runs through the spoken narrative of all these people.

I was born in Madras, and some four decades later find myself a resident of Chennai. Many of us who live here often come up against the assumption that it is for lack of opportunities elsewhere. To the contrary, many of its citizens who have the resources to live anywhere in the world *choose* to live here.

For long, visitors to the city thought of it as sleepy, not-'happening', backward even in its conservative attitudes. 'There's *nothing* to do here,' was the common complaint. What they missed was that it was a place that allowed one to *be*, a place that emphasized the inner life. It is a secret its inhabitants have kept for a very long time, choosing, with their characteristic modesty, not to broadcast it loudly. It was only a matter of time before the secret was discovered; recently *The New York Times* included Chennai in its list of 52 places to visit in 2014 and *Lonely Planet* listed it as one of ten best cities to visit in 2015.

My parents, both of whom had grown up in Uttar Pradesh, had moved to Madras in the late sixties. Not given to rituals or its newer forms – going to the movie-theatre, watching cricket – ours was a home that relied heavily on books for entertainment and community. It was in my friends' homes that I discovered the grand procession of festivals and celebrations. I also learnt that I was from elsewhere, different. But when I headed to Delhi with my mother, every summer and winter, to spend the vacations at my grandparents' home, I was even more an outsider. If my Gujarati grandmother teased me for being a Madrasi, it didn't really matter, I knew I was all the richer for having assimilated Tamil culture.

And it is from this immersion, both as insider and outsider, that this book has been written.

Tulsi Badrinath

Chennai
October 2014

1

The Individual and the Collective

'Once I got my black belt, my father was reassured.'
K Seshadri

The childhood memory – of snake shrines and light dancing on a wick – continues to represent the city to me.

The road where the shrine once existed ended in a T-junction. At the time, there was an empty plot of land beyond. In this city, it is inauspicious to own land that directly faces a road running perpendicular to it. Soon most of the vacant plots were bought up and houses built, but this one remained vacant for a long time, filling up with water when it rained and resounding with the cacophony of croaking frogs.

When people did buy it, the first thing they did was build a miniature alcove for Ganesha in their compound wall. The god was installed with due ceremony to preside over the converging roads. Thereafter in the evenings, on approaching the T-junction, one saw a flame lit to the elephant-headed god.

Across neighbourhoods, there are many such three-way intersections where, appeased by incense and lamp light, Ganesha protects one. And before darkness falls, women hurry to light a lamp in their homes.

On the full moon night in the Tamil month of Krithigai, around mid-November, the members of a household painstakingly twirl wicks and immerse them in oil-filled brass and earthen lamps of all shapes and sizes. In millions of dwellings, hut or bungalow, beautiful clusters of light are visible at the doorstep, and rows of lamps over walls and gates. More than Deepavali, this is the festival of lights across the state, a celebration that has continued for more than 2,000 years. Walking down the road at dusk, one rejoices in the display of radiance unique to each home.

When a spot has attracted worship, and when people are convinced there are powerful energies around, then before long they collect money to build a more permanent shelter, gifting the deity the modern conveniences of lights, fans, running water and more elaborate rituals. At various places one can see these shrines, smaller than temples, but larger than the rudimentary stone or anthill installations. In an incongruous if amusing development, very often their inner walls are covered with plain ceramic bathroom tiles which are convenient to clean. The Tamil mind is practical above all.

Which particular shrine attracts one's faith depends on a connection forged with that particular energy and one's own precarious state of being. Right near the Adyar Post Office, there is a little temple to Ganesha, and I remember, in the days before the internet, addressing a prayer to him before sending the manuscript of my first novel to various publishers. There is one that I am yet to visit: a shrine dedicated to Cricket Ganesha, where the deity – bowler, batsman, team eleven all-rounder – intervenes in cricket matches assuring India a win such as that in the India-Australia match in 2001.

While the ancient temples at Triplicane and Mylapore existed centuries before Madras did, Madras acquired its own temple, the Chenna Kesava Perumal temple or Great Pagoda, soon after its birth. It is befitting that coins minted by the East India Company not only bore the image of a temple tower but were also called *pagodas*. When the Company decided to demolish much of the original Black Town, Great

Pagoda included, and resettle it further inland, they offered to help build another temple as recompense. Given the natural propensity of this soil to generate temples, what was to have been one became two – the Chenna Kesava temple and the Chenna Mallikeswara temple. One for Vishnu, the other for Shiva.

It is in a temple, dedicated to Kalikambal, that we find a record of Chatrapati Shivaji's visit to the area in 1677. And it was in the Parthasarathy temple that poet-patriot Subramania Bharati was flung to the ground by an elephant. Many hundreds of places of worship, of which some of the more famous are the Kapaleeshwarar and Sri Ramakrishna Universal temples, the Velankanni church, the Wallajah and Thousand Lights mosques, the Agiary in Royapuram, the Jain Mandir and Gurudwara in T Nagar, dot the city.

In the mornings, office-goers offer a drive-by salute to the gods, while some stop their bikes for a minute to register their presence. If you happen to be driving at the time, either you stop too for a fraction of a second, seeking a glimpse of the deity, seeking benediction, or you curse the stalled traffic around these shrines. In the evenings, it is freshly dressed women with their children who crowd around the narrow doorway.

The gods are forgetful; they need daily reminders of one's existential dilemmas.

At the time the Ashtalakshmi temple was built, in 1976, it was situated on the outer periphery of the city. I remember visiting it as a child when it was sanctified by ritual but not yet energized by faith. It did not enclose vast stretches of land as do the great temples of Tamil Nadu, and had only one outer *prakara* or corridor for circumambulation around the deity. In this, in the bright synthetic paint that coated the mythological figures on its modest *vimana* or central dome, in the absence of a square tank of water, in the eight sancta that rose high up in the air, clustered over three levels, it proclaimed its newness, and urban origins.

Returning after decades, I stopped to buy offerings. Only those with a purpose – visiting the temple or beach, or returning home – would venture onto this road for it ends suddenly, yielding to sand, a few catamarans, and the restless haze of sea. There are not too many shops on this stretch, apart from the usual stalls that front any temple, selling coconuts, bananas and garlands.

The flower seller deftly, if disinterestedly, smoothed open the pink petals of seven lotus buds, arranged them in a cane basket, and then placed a beautiful white one atop. Walking past the wall painted in broad stripes of red and white, I stepped barefoot into the complex.

I love visiting temples, and today was no different. There were hardly any people there. I zipped through the maze of dividers meant for crowd control, their ugly utilitarian steel at variance with the curving lines of the temple architecture.

Soon I beheld the Chief Goddess of the temple, Mahalakshmi herself. I stood very close to her, my eyes intent on her smiling face. The sheen on her skin of smooth black stone, the dazzle of gems, the blaze of her red silk sari all coalesced into a shimmering parabola beneath that orb. In seconds, a compact was made by sight between grace and plea, between deity and devotee. Minutes later, I registered the taller crowned figure standing beside her, brocaded cotton clothing his lower half, the off-white cool against his black torso. The mark on his forehead, a single line of rubies held within a U of white diamonds, proclaimed him Vishnu.

When the temple was dreamt of, literally, by a well-known priest, it was conceived as a temple for eight Lakshmis and accordingly, their images were made. A little later, realizing that the Great One required her consort with her, an image of Mahavishnu was commissioned as well. In the main sanctum, they presided together assuring me of Benevolent Protection and Prosperity, while in her other seven forms, the Goddess reigned with supreme self-confidence by herself.

Two priests moved about in the inner sanctum, within the raised threshold that demarcated the space as exclusive to them. The distinctive tuft of hair on an otherwise shaven head, a limp discoloured cotton thread falling aslant from the left shoulder across a chest damp with sweat, with traditional gold earrings weighty in their earlobes, yards of cloth draping their lower bodies, their very appearance announced both their orthodoxy and profession. Above all, it was the gleaming *thiruman* decorating their forehead, the U of clay, bearing a vertical yellow line within that proudly announced their devotion to Vishnu.

I had come to meet one of them, the one with a kindly face. Lean of body, about fifty years of age, the bristles that covered his cheeks were salt-and-pepper. His name was Seshadri and he had briefly found fame for an unusual pursuit.

As I held my basket aloft, Seshadri took the white lotus and tucked it into the folds of the Devi's sari. Others' offerings were similarly conveyed to the deity before a camphor flame was waved in a circle around her. As the priest turned away from her, bearing the brass plate with the flame, I stretched my palm over it, feeling the barely palpable warmth momentarily before other anxious hands edged mine out. To miss contact with the flame, even if it was a notional gesture from afar, was to feel that blessings had passed one by, to feel a little bereft; no one wanted that. As Seshadri furrowed through the crowd, the sound of coins dropping on the plate preceded him.

Arranging to visit Seshadri later, I climbed the steep steps of a dark, narrow staircase that led to the sister shrines of the other Lakshmis. A little later, descending from the top-most shrine, I was suddenly out in the open but still at a height, facing the limitless sea, its teal blue waves edged with froth. I realized then that it served in place of the usual temple tank for this sea-born Goddess, who had risen in all her beauty from the ocean when it was churned by the gods and the demons aeons ago.

I left the temple clutching the kumkum that had been dropped into my palm, a smidgen at a time, at each of the eight shrines. It was a sacred souvenir, not to be dusted off, but preserved. Many paper pellets of vermillion, collected from numerous temples, filled the inner pockets of my purses and handbags with the promise of grand and imminent luck. But today I had nothing to fold it into; I rubbed as much as I could onto my forehead and opened my palm, stained turmeric-yellow by now, guiltily to the breeze.

Seshadri lived close to the temple, on the first floor of a low building fronting the temple-street. More steep steps rising into the gloom later, I found myself at his front door. When I had first read about Seshadri, long before I thought about writing this book, he seemed to exemplify to me the people of this city, who held firm to tradition but were also in step with modern times. Seshadri was a black belt in karate, pursuing his contrary – even forbidden – passion, while simultaneously adhering to his life of orthodox, and scrupulous, ritual.

Now, seated cross-legged on the floor, though he offered me a seat on one of the plastic chairs stacked in a corner of his living room cum kitchen, I was face to face with the Karate Priest, or Japan Iyer, as inhabitants of the predominantly fisherfolk locality call him. There was a certain spareness about him, and something gentle as well. His wife Vijayalakshmi, more rotund than he, stood listening. When he spoke, he glanced at her as well, anxious to include her in the conversation. I observed what I had missed earlier in the temple, the delicate mark of Vishnu that decorated not only his forehead but the sides of his throat, his chest and his forearms.

Seshadri remembered how it had shaped his childhood. 'My grandfather said we should bear the sign of Vishnu at all times, so that when He came to check on us, He would be pleased. Each night, I would re-apply it and then wait excitedly for Perumal to appear before I fell asleep.'

The second child of Aaviyur Krishnamachari, Seshadri grew up in the small town of Thirukoilur. His father would wake him up at the pre-dawn hour to do yogasanas, and recite the Vedas. Krishnamachari himself had been trained as a priest by *his* father who, since his siblings had all variously joined the military, banks, or worked as accountants, wanted to ensure that at least one branch of the family maintained its tradition.

Krishnamachari served as a priest in a temple at Mayavaram. He was an expert in the Agamas that delineate temple rituals and in the Sanskrit language. He believed that exercise was important for health; he lifted weights; did yoga. On Friday nights, wearing a shirt for protection against the wind, though otherwise stitched cloth was forbidden to him, he would cycle the 150 kilometres between Mayavaram and Thirukoilur, reaching home at dawn on Saturday morning. When invited to serve in the newly built Ashtalakshmi temple, he had moved with his family to Madras.

Seshadri explained, 'In the village, you won't get work whereas in the city there are more people who call one to perform ceremonies. So a lot of Brahmins have come away to the city.' His father had enrolled him in a government-run school, in nearby Besant Nagar.

Young Seshadri was quite daring. One day, when his brother was carrying a bag of coins, their father's income from the *arati* plate, a ruffian snatched it and ran away. *A weak Iyer is no threat*, was probably the thief's assessment. He hadn't taken into account Seshadri, who set out in search of him. Finding the thief perched some distance away on a rickshaw smoking a *beedi*, Seshadri knocked him to the ground and triumphantly retrieved the bag of coins. The amount was handed over at Tamil Nadu Stores – run by a Muslim who was their friend and gave them provisions on easy terms of credit – and the amount credited to their family's account, a fact that Seshadri reported proudly to his father. 'I had no fear then, but now, after marriage, I worry, about my children … family.' In the old-fashioned way, it was an oblique reference to his wife.

An invigorating fragrance spread through the room. Vijayalakshmi was brewing filter coffee in the kitchen, separated from the room by a narrow wall. Distracted by the aroma, I had to summon all my attention to listen to Seshadri.

One day in 1993, struck by the karate bug while watching it on television, he had decided to learn the art of self-defence. He was, by now, a grown man. Having spent eight years in Calcutta working as a priest in one temple while his father served in another, Seshadri had travelled to many parts of north India, wherever he was invited to perform rites. Father and son had returned to Madras, to serve the Goddess at her temple. What would have been an innocuous desire for anyone else – wanting to learn karate – brought Seshadri full tilt into conflict with the way of life he had been born into, its world view.

'Don't learn it,' forbade his father, angrily. 'I'll teach you more yoga if you like. This is going to interfere with your spiritual growth. As a priest you must enhance your sattva or quality of peace, not go towards the restless and rousing *rajoguna*.' There was the question of the tunic and trousers used for practice – stitched, therefore forbidden. There was the fear that a different, heartier diet may be required. There was also the fear that Seshadri would mix with people whose influence was undesirable.

Living in a close-knit community with a wide network of relatives, working in a temple where one was watched closely for signs of deviance by jealous others, Seshadri could not breach boundaries with impunity. When the temple watchman suggested a karate class nearby that was fast becoming popular, Seshadri hesitated. Word would spread, his father would come to know, and he really did not have the audacity to wear the *karate gi*, the white uniform, in full public view.

An uncle of his helped out, suggesting a coach named Dayalan, with the Crime Branch Division of the CID, who lived in Mayavaram. Dayalan was astounded when Seshadri approached him, had his own doubts about a thin, curd-rice eating Brahmin having what it took – 'I will teach you but will you be able to bear the rigour, Swami?' – but agreed to teach him and even waived the requirement of a uniform. 'You will come here only four days a month so you *must* practice in Chennai,' was his only rule. Every fifteen days, Seshadri would tell his father that his uncle had summoned him and leave the city for his classes.

Stripped to the tiniest piece of cloth and the single *namam* on his forehead, Seshadri engaged in gruelling sessions with Dayalan. Leaving his uncle's house at four-thirty in the morning, he would return late in the evening. Having to follow the rules of pollution meant he had to carry his food *and* water with him. 'I got to rest every half hour. It was very hard work. Dayalan was a little worried that he might get into trouble for teaching me ... but when I learnt wholeheartedly from him he was very happy. He took a great interest in me. I proved to him that a vegetarian can also be strong.'

Back in Chennai, Seshadri woke well before dawn, to run 20 kilometres along the beach. At that still hour of darkness, he wore shorts, jogging shoes and a cap over his *kudumi* or knotted tuft of hair. Only his ear-studs would give him away if someone were to see him. His dedication resulted in his winning many prizes in karate competitions and soon he was written about in the iconic *Ananda Vikatan* magazine. In most homes, family members vied with each other to lay their hands on the latest issue of the wildly popular Tamil magazine. Krishnamachari was stunned when he read about his son in it.

'First he was upset. But then, he slowly understood that it was a good thing ... he was happy that I was praised. He told me that earlier he had not known there was this scope in it, and that because the two lines of activity were so different, he was worried on my behalf. Also, he had won renown as a great scholar, so to have his son doing this ... But once I got my black belt, and everyone praised me, he was reassured.' The community too accepted Seshadri's passion for karate.

Seshadri moved up the levels in his proficiency at karate, and took up kick-boxing as well. He spent hours watching Bruce Lee's every move, analysing the flow of movement, the acute intelligence directing each kick. He was selected for competitions abroad, but that involved a terrible choice. To cross the seven seas or not. 'I did not go, because there was no *prayaschittam*, no atonement by ritual. My livelihood as a priest would have been affected, my thread would have been wasted, so I did not go for the tournaments.'

He began to teach karate and many parents also sent their daughters to learn. Now when he went for his morning jog people would stop him to congratulate him. However, he limited his scope, concentrating on his work as a priest. 'Maybe if I had started a school to teach karate I would have earned a lot too. But my work and karma is this. This is my path – knowledge of the Vedas and rituals, belonging to an orthodox family of priests, Brahmana.'

Seshadri's wife served me some frothy coffee, in the twin tumbler-*dabara* set. It was piping hot. Cooling some in the dabara dish, given for that purpose, I transferred it back to the tumbler, before tilting my head back so as to pour a little coffee into my mouth. I had to remind myself that to sip from the tumbler would be to pollute it.

Even this – 'filter coffee' – something ubiquitous in most Brahmin homes, was frowned upon as a beverage in the early part of the century. Seshadri himself did not remember his grandparents ever drinking it. But it had conquered all resistance, and the two-chamber filter took pride of place in the kitchen as the decoction had to be brewed in a timely manner. An increase in coffee prices usually creates a disproportionate crisis in many a family budget, unlike that of vegetables which can be substituted one for another.

In 2003, continued Seshadri, came what seemed like the chance of a lifetime. The officer in charge of all security at the Tirumala Tirupati Devasthanam (TTD), that temple of temples, read about Seshadri and, in what can only be described as an inspired moment, thought that it might be worthwhile teaching the priests there karate for self-defence. Officials were dispatched to Madras to meet Seshadri and then he was invited to Tirupati for further discussions. The idea was to train young priests between the age of eighteen and twenty-four, and post them in three shifts in the inner sanctum. Should any terrorist breach all the security and get in, the priests would form the last line of defence.

Needless to say, Seshadri was overwhelmed. His father had once advised him about karate, 'Do not let this come in the way of your service to Perumal. He is our All. Everything we do is for Him. He is the one who looks after us.' And now this very karate would be used to serve Perumal.

In Tirupati, Seshadri was sent straight into the sanctum ahead of the queue, a blessing in itself, and told that he could stay as long as he liked. That was abundance! The impact of Tirupati Balaji on one's soul is indelible even in the brief seconds-long darshan one normally gets. Seshadri stood to one side of the sanctum for over three hours, dazzled by the Lord, overcome by emotion. The strict rules concerning the rites meant he could not officiate there as a priest, but could gaze at that striking figure and imbibe blessings by sight to his heart's content.

Later, discussions involving his terms of service were held. It was all very tempting – residential quarters, free education for his son and daughter, his own jeep, a walkie-talkie and the proximity of Perumal, but Seshadri had only one request – that his job be made permanent. That was not possible, they said, offering him a two-year contract. He had served at the Mahalakshmi temple for fifteen years and was apprehensive about having nothing to fall back on after the contract expired. Perhaps he could come to Tirupati on deputation, he suggested humbly.

When he got back home, he was famous. The major Indian television networks, the BBC, Tamil and English news publications, they all featured his story. Somehow the news had leaked about the TTD's invitation. Just as suddenly as Seshadri was all over the news, the TTD did not take the proposal forward. It fizzled out.

'Thayar could not bear to let you go,' I burst out, referring to his 'boss' in Madras, the Goddess Mahalakshmi, also

Perumal's wife. It must have been a major disappointment, but Seshadri spoke of it philosophically. 'Yes, Perumal called me, but Thayar kept me here.'

That brief exposure to fame however was to again create controversy. Avoidable, as it exposed him to petty politics and jealousy. He was told not to do public interviews, and asked to get permission from the temple authorities before doing so. 'It has to do with karate, my personal life, and it does not affect my carrying out my duties as a priest in any way,' protested Seshadri.

Many changes had happened in the years since the temple was built. It was no longer 'new' but still novel, well amalgamated into the city proper, and a popular destination presenting as it did opportunity for both a pilgrimage and an outing to the beach. Bounded forever by the shoreline, the city has expanded far beyond in the other directions. But chiefly, the temple itself, originally run by volunteers and trustees, had been entrusted to the government in 1992 and was subject to the rules of the Hindu Religious and Charitable Endowments Department. Therefore, Seshadri could invoke them. 'Show me the government order that says I can't do physical exercise, and I'll stop,' he shot back. Even so, he was careful. Most of the television footage about him was taken at other temples, ones that allowed him leeway.

Seshadri led me up a steep staircase to a terrace that served as the entrance to another tenant's home. There are no steps leading up to the 'bald' roof, and he has to almost climb parkour to reach it at dawn when he practices. There was no way I could reach it without a ladder.

We stood on the first floor terrace, the colourful vimana of the temple rising high into the sky from this vantage point. It was a rare view, both for its proximity and its perspective.

It also emphasized the temple's centrality in his life. Seshadri's day is bound by do-s and don't-s. So many of them are privately observed that it takes fidelity and commitment to honour them. The primary temptation really is to cheat, and Seshadri knows many priests who negotiate with cunning the strict rules.

It is not easy, in a city that has seen virulent anti-Brahmin feeling. While others in his community have adopted the anonymous shirt-pant and work in offices (some maintaining their scrupulosity regarding food and drink), Seshadri in attire and appearance necessarily displays his caste. While growing up in Madras, he was teased by the urchins near the temple, both for his tuft and the sacred thread. 'Now it has changed,' he said. 'They no longer pass comments. I go everywhere dressed like this, though I do wear a shirt. In Calcutta, I did not even need the shirt while travelling by bus, they had so much respect for priests like us.' He observed that the children in the slum nearby had been educated and some had become engineers or had got good government jobs, bettering their economic status, so they were more accepting now, approaching him for help with pujas or medicine or choosing auspicious dates for ceremonies.

He still wakes at 4 a.m., spends two hours on his karate-linked fitness, and must bathe in time for sunrise, when it is time for the *sandhya* ritual guarding the junction of night and day. Unless he does this ceremony, personally, thrice a day, his work at the temple would not be fruitful. 'I *have* to do everything at the given time. Because it is regular, it has become easy over the years. If I do the sandhya late, because I got late returning from the temple, I have to do the associated penance.'

The temple opens at eight-thirty in the morning and if he is on duty, Seshadri's tasks involve opening the doors to the shrine, cleaning it, tidying the garments worn by the deities, lighting the lamp and being ready to receive offerings. 'I won't sit vacant-minded there. I keep chanting mantras in my head.' There are pujas which have to be done at a certain time, decorations and dressing of the deities, and Seshadri can return home at noon for some rest before heading back at 3.45 p.m. The temple closes for the day at eight-thirty in the night, and he sleeps early.

The temple is crowded on Fridays, the day beloved of the Goddess. Similarly, the nine nights when the Goddess is worshipped, Navaratri; that one moonless night when Mahalakshmi comes visiting, Deepavali; and the Fridays in the month of Thai are all special. These follow the traditional Indian lunar calendar. But January 1st, the *other* New Year, from the Gregorian calendar has also become a time to visit the gods; start the year well. 'Now on New Year's Day there is a huge crowd! As per the shastras, we cannot open the temple before 4 a.m., so they stream in as soon as we open the gates!'

There is no leave; he serves the Goddess 365 days a year.

He cannot eat out at any joint. Certain vegetables and tubers such as onion, garlic, beans or the drumstick are not allowed. Water for drinking must be pumped from the ground or a well; no tap water. When carried on travels, it cannot be contained in plastic or steel. Only in silver or brass, and for further protection wrapped in silk. Should he sleep during the day, he must bathe before entering the temple; should he travel by bus, he must bathe on reaching home. These are just some of the prohibitions related to purity and pollution that regulate his life.

When Seshadri first bought a bike, it helped avoid the accidental pollution inherent in bus travel. For example, he might rub shoulders with someone returning from a funeral and therefore ritually impure. The bike was to unleash another passion in him; over the years he has owned over twenty vehicles of all sorts. From the sturdy Bullet, the equally sturdy Java, and the sleek Yamaha RX 100, Seshadri has enjoyed them all.

As he revealed this aspect of himself, I was secretly amused. If there is one sight in the city that captures everyone's imagination including mine, it is the almost anachronistic sight of a very orthodox Brahmin riding the latest bike, a waist-pack – of nylon, therefore acceptable – settled on his belly, hair-tuft streaming in the wind. And here in Seshadri I had found one such.

His love affair with vehicles then moved up a notch. Requiring a larger vehicle to ferry his growing children, Seshadri bought an auto-rickshaw for Rs 15,000. Painted blue, it signalled that it was for private use. When the driver he hired turned out to be a drunk, enterprising Seshadri decided to drive it himself. 'I'm known as the only priest who's owned an auto. When my father came to visit, I would pick him up from Central station in my auto. I once drove it 200 kilometres. My wife, the children and food, they were all packed in the back and I drove!' Now Seshadri has graduated to a car, an Alto.

He taught both his children karate, and his college-going, football playing son is a brown belt. Though his son has been trained by Seshadri in the rituals, most probably he will get a job somewhere after earning his college degree. His daughter is proficient in yoga.

Relishing the unexpected and open view of the sea, the temple tower and some huts in the distance, I peered over the parapet wall. For Seshadri, the road below anchors his life, linking his place of work and his home in the tenement opposite. This location, so convenient otherwise, had brought torment one December, in 2004.

He had left early in the morning with some other priests, all heading to a temple near Villupuram, some three hours away. It was the kind of work that brought good extra income, ceremonies requiring an assembly of priests. Quite some distance into the journey they received terrible news. *There is no Madras, nothing. A tsunami came and the waves travelled five kilometres inland. Everything has been destroyed. There is no Mahalakshmi temple. Nothing remains.*

'I thought of my wife, my two children. I wept...' Tears welled in his eyes. 'See, now too I am crying. I cried to Perumal, "I have come to see you and you have taken my family." There was no way to contact them; the phone kept ringing. I spoke to another relative who said the temple was untouched ... After all, *She* is the daughter of the ocean, so it would not trouble *Her*. I told him to arrange for a car and go in search of my family. I wanted to return home. The others priests accompanying me said, "What will be achieved if you go back? Nothing. You have come this far, finish your work."'

Tears flowed as he remembered past distress. Listening to him, I was moved. 'I had no choice but to complete my journey. In the temple, I fell at Perumal's feet and told him, "I have come to serve you, I will fulfill all your wishes, now please look after my family. Trusting you, I left them in *your* care. Only you can help me." It was only four hours later, around noon that his wife managed to call him; she had grabbed her children, whatever money she could and had waded through the street filled with sea water and debris to safety. Seshadri returned to Madras by bike at 10 p.m. that night. 'By then it was all over. All the thatched huts had collapsed. The boats were slammed inland. But the waters had only reached the steps of the temple, and ... my family was safe!'

We returned downstairs, to the cramped hall where posters of Bruce Lee and colourful calendars hung alongside the all-important *panchangam* or almanac. 'Almost half my income goes towards rent,' revealed Seshadri. It took a long struggle to get a monthly salary sanctioned by the government. Before that, his income relied solely on the collections from the arati plate, shared between seven priests on rotation at the main and other shrines. In a good month, he earns about Rs 10,000. Sometimes an NRI might drop a 100 dollar bill or South African rands and there is the excitement of a transaction in foreign currency. He has no pension to look forward to, no health benefits.

'Step by step,' Seshadri has saved what he can. When an opportunity arose, he bought a small plot of land to the south-west of the city, near Pallavaram and the airport. In time, as the metropolis expanded to touch far-off Polichalur, with a temple dating back to the ninth century, his investment has proved solid. 'I've built a small house there, which follows the requirements of the shastras – a long hall with no bedroom as such, just like in the village. The puja is in the kitchen, to ensure that we offer every speck of food to Perumal before consuming it.'

Mud floors in village homes were washed with cowdung, valued for its antiseptic properties when fully dry. In Seshadri's new home, 'the floor is tiled, but a ritual smearing with cow-dung and turmeric of the area where food is sanctified ensures ritual-purity. We wipe it off afterwards. The Indian-style toilet is built at a distance from the main building.' Practicality and a willingness to adapt are evident here as well. 'I've also built a western-style toilet with a commode, should we ever need it in old age when we are infirm.'

When he can no longer serve in the temple, Seshadri plans to shift to his own home. 'I will continue to conduct pujas and teach karate. If Perumal gives me ten rupees, I am happy.'

2

Power of the Pen

'Many castes intermingle in the city.'
P Sivakami

When asked which cadre he would like to belong to, my father, newly inducted into the IAS, had chosen Tamil Nadu on a whim. 'I did not know much about the south, I thought it would be a good way to learn,' he explained to me later. This resulted in his shifting to Madras, far away from his native Uttar Pradesh.

Growing up in Madras, answering the questions we Indians delight in asking, I understood my family did not follow many conventions.

'Name?' was the primary guide to caste.

Only, my father, wanting to discard all overt signs, had not only given up wearing his sacred thread but also the use of his community-indicative surname. For a while he called himself just Badrinath. Later, understanding that dropping part of one's name was no solution to the inequities of caste, and inspired by the Tamil practice of stating one's village and ancestry first and then one's name, he reversed his name to Chaturvedi Badrinath.

He also gave me his name as my surname, which both erased the direct connection to our community and led people to assume that I was Iyengar, or perhaps even Kannadiga.

'Mother tongue?' That was a tough one. My mother was half Gujarati and half Maharashtrian, but since she had grown up in Uttar Pradesh, Hindi was the language she was more familiar with. When asked in school, I would answer 'Braj bhasha', the dialect my paternal aunts spoke – to me incomprehensible – and the entire class, perennially hungry, would dissolve in laughter: 'Bread Badusha!' Similarly, native place morphed from unheard of Mainpuri, near Agra, into Manipuri.

In a city where caste still mattered, more than in the other three major metros, and where its dynamics came into subtle play in day to day interactions, to be an outsider meant one had to negotiate these boundaries with care. The primary identity and group dynamics of caste are still deeply embedded here. In clothing, language, register, food, attitudes and traditions they are visible, reinforced, but these markers are not easily apparent to a tourist or temporary visitor to the city. And they are but a culmination of centuries of rigid demarcations between Brahmins and non-Brahmins, 'upper' and 'lower' castes.

Significantly, it was in all-too-traditional Madras that many radical voices were raised against caste-linked practices and prejudice. EV Ramasamy, simply known as Periyar, was perhaps the most influential. Born at the end of the nineteenth century, he both witnessed and experienced the caste-sanctioned arrogance of Brahmins. While Kerala took the idea of pollution by a Dalit to an extreme – not only did they have to maintain a certain distance from the higher castes, call out in warning if they were in the vicinity, even the sight of them was enough to pollute a Namboodiri – Tamil Nadu was not far behind. Over the course of his long life of about ninety-four years, Periyar fought to dismantle those social structures that allowed it to thrive.

The Self-Respect Movement aimed at raising the self-esteem of non-Brahmins, the dropping of caste surnames, the Justice Party's battle against the economic and political power of Brahmins, the Anti-Hindi agitations of 1938, 1948, 1952 and 1965, the birth of the Dravida Kazhagam, the insistence on rights for women, the conducting of marriages without Brahmin priests and Vedic rituals, the pride in Tamil and the eradication of untouchability – these were just some of the social reforms supported by Periyar.

Even the two main political parties, the DMK and the AIADMK, were born of the Dravida Kazhagam. If the DMK split from the DK because it wanted to remain part of the Indian nation while still carrying out the reforms envisioned by Periyar, the AIADMK split from the DMK because of differences of opinion between M Karunanidhi, leader of the DMK, and MG Ramachandran. Importantly, they provided a regional alternative to the Congress Party, while also achieving a presence in national politics. Indeed, after the anti-Hindi agitations of 1965, the Congress never came back to power in Tamil Nadu.

For the longest time, before the Supreme Court ban of 2008, red and black DMK flags, or banners bearing the two-leaves symbol of the AIADMK were aflutter all over the city. Streamers stretched in a canopy over roads, towering cut-outs of the major political leaders popped up along pavements, and posters were stuck on every available flat surface. To travel down a road was to absorb a constant stream of colour from the corner of one's eye, the gold of the sun rising between two black mountains, the green of leaves and the dazzle of white from the shirt and *veshti* politicians unfailingly wore.

People often separate Chennai from the earlier sleepy Madras as the city of malls and branded boutiques, of 'happening' cafes and restaurants, of posh cars and the soon to be inaugurated Metro rail, of gyms and discotheques, but ancient prejudices and oppression continue to throb below the surface.

In fact, one might say that caste tensions have increased visibly in the state, going by the furious, often violent, opposition to inter-caste marriages.

Chiefly, most of the political parties have relied on caste-based vote banks, both asserting and hardening the boundaries of caste, without doing much for a wider integration of Dalits. 'While most castes have made progress after the nation's independence, a few, particularly Dalits, have not made commendable progress. Continued oppression by other castes is one of the reasons for the same,' said P Sivakami while releasing a book recently.

In the person of Sivakami, two features that can form a double disadvantage – Dalit and female – combine to create someone who has risen from a background of poverty to occupy a seat of power. As an IAS officer, Sivakami was not only in a position to actually implement change, but also help the poor and dispossessed. As a writer, she has added to the literature of the country detailing the Dalit experience.

I drove south of the city towards her house in Palavakkam, glad it was afternoon and there was less traffic. The road that became the East Coast Road further ahead is notorious for the number of people that die in accidents at night, seduced by the long stretch of well-tarred surface into speeding.

The East Coast Road links Madras with Pondicherry. When the outer limits of the city have been left behind, the scenery is all silvery-blue and green; vast stretches of sea waves and casuarina trees. Backwaters glitter in the sun, salt lies heaped in mounds and men work on half-finished boats along the picturesque route that passes through many villages, whose thatch-roofed or single-storey cement homes are surrounded by coconut groves and paddy fields. What to me, and most travellers, seemed idyllic, was to Sivakami the constricting locus, in village after village, where caste oppression had been practised for centuries.

But I was still within the limits of the city, crossing localities along the coast that were engulfed by the city's voracious appetite for space and land. There were many reminders of its village origins, in the rows of small shops operated by petty traders, in the nature of the dimly lit shops themselves: tyre-repair, metal forging, groceries sold in small quantities, medicinal herbs, hardware, paints, coffee freshly ground in a small mill, and 'variety' stores that offered an assortment of fancy things from cheap nail polish, safety pins and hair clips to brown paper for school textbooks. Their signage was hand-painted and the names local.

As I drove, I could see a different kind of commercial establishment had erupted in the midst of the old, with its neon lettering and glass-fronted exteriors. These were franchises of big brands, both Indian and international. And here, as I left the city further behind, it was clear more than elsewhere that a certain part of the population would never venture into these spaces, barred by poverty and lack of entitlement.

But the person I was going to meet, Sivakami, had made the reverse journey, some thirty years ago. A journey from a village in interior Tamil Nadu, Perambalur near Trichy, all the way to the fabled city 'Patnam' or Madras, and within that to preside over lives while holding a government office.

Soon, I was at her gate, praying that its metal would protect me from the dog barking on the other side. Dog secured, maid immensely amused, I was led into a big drawing room of a spacious double-storeyed house. As I waited, I had time to observe the portraits of Buddha and Dr Ambedkar that hung side by side on one wall. On another wall, in a niche, stood a tall bronze of Shiva as Ardhanarishwara, below a Tanjore painting of a baby Krishna.

Sivakami entered the room, her hair freshly washed, mahogany skin gleaming. We began our conversation with the earliest memory she had of Madras. 'I woke up in a studio dazzled by the lights, and I remember asking for some sweets. I was about ten years old. My father used to visit Madras quite often and he had brought us along. I was sick and could not go sight-seeing with my siblings, so my father had arranged to take me to the film studio to make up for it.'

In the mid-seventies, Sivakami returned to Madras, to study in Queen Mary's College, right on the promenade of Marina Beach. 'I stayed in the Presidency Women's College hostel adjacent to the state guest house on Wallajah Road. I loved those days. On weekday mornings, I would take a bus from Chepauk to Queen Mary's enjoying the sight of the sea to my left. In the evenings I would walk back to the hostel, savouring the sea breeze on my skin. It was not so crowded then. We had to get back by 6 p.m.! It was only on the weekends that we had time to go to the beach.

'North Madras,' continued Sivakami, 'I did not visit as much but it is the original nucleus of the city. There were no proper parks there, it was very crowded. One rarely found bungalows with gardens. Though the land prices were high in the commercial part, it was really the poor and lower middle class who lived there. Of course, the areas everyone was most familiar with were the busy commercial part near Parry's corner, China Bazaar for textiles, and Burma Bazaar for smuggled goods … the small gullies and lots of shops. But there was a vast difference between north and south Madras. The two parts of the city were almost like two different worlds.'

North Madras continues to lag behind in development, while the city prefers to grow in the southern direction.

As to the population, continued Sivakami, 'They say that Madras was mostly inhabited by Dalits earlier, north Madras especially, so the Mayor of the city used to be Dalit. The main areas where they lived were Chetpet, Saidapet, Thousand Lights, Poonga Nagar, opposite the Collectorate and near the harbour, in Kasimedu.'

The harbour itself, built from 1881 onwards, is a walled kingdom unto itself. It guards the maritime approach to the city but also benefits from free access to the waves. The story is that almost everyone who works there has two wives, they make that much money ... On the day that salaries are paid, a lot of women wait at the gate to collect money from their husbands, before it is spent elsewhere. It is not surprising that Burma Bazaar, where all sorts of contraband can be procured for a price, is situated right near the port.

Sivakami talked about the chief thrills offered by the city when she was a student – a visit to the zoo, the museum and the cinema. 'In the village, it can be suffocating. One can't loiter.' Along with the anonymity granted by the city, the excellent network of PTC buses, with seats along the length of one side reserved for women, allowed her to travel in relative ease. In fact, it gave the young girl an opportunity to observe that 'buses and trains are open to all castes. No segregation by caste in the living areas. Madras city has a good mix of people and facilities are common to all, by and large.' Further, that 'urbanization is a good way to breach the caste structure because one isn't bound by caste identity here and many castes intermingle in the city.'

But one day, while getting off a bus near Kannagi statue, she had her first experience of 'eve-teasing'. 'Someone called out to me "Sister, sister. Just check your buttons!" I was wearing a back-buttoned blouse. I twisted my neck and looked. It was all okay. I was paralyzed. Why did he do that to me? He vanished.'

Next time it was worse. When someone felt her up in the bus, she shouted at him. 'A fat woman came to *his* rescue. "You look so ugly and you are complaining about this boy. Take a taxi instead!" This would not have happened in the village. Everyone knows who is who.'

Undeterred, she continued to use the bus on outings. 'As students, we were not so rich to go to hotels such as Chola which charged thirty rupees a buffet.' Instead, she and her classmates enjoyed the 'full special meal' at Woodlands which cost only five rupees. At farewell gatherings held at Woodlands Drive-in or Hotel Maris, there was the 'thrill of bumping into boys from boys' colleges'. The furthest she ventured was some ten kilometres away to Besant Nagar to visit the Ashtalakshmi temple.

'Madras ended at Adyar. Everything else was beyond.' To plan a trip to Mahabalipuram, sixty kilometres away, was to embark on an adventure. Catching glimpses of the sea as one drove parallel to it, en route to the ancient port city, was to pass villages not considered part of the city at the time. 'Just crossing Thiruvanmiyur seemed like a big distance. Kottivakkam was more of a fisherman's colony. Palavakkam where I live now was insignificant. Neelankarai still had blue lilies in a big temple tank and the sand on the beach was so golden. Cholamandal Artists' Village was filled with casuarina trees.' Today, all these areas have a considerable population.

Further down was the biggest attraction, VGP beach resort, filled with small-town visitors eager to see its surreal landscape of larger-than-life cement sculptures and cheered by the imminent possibility of watching famous heroes and heroines shoot even more surreal song sequences. Having seen that pavilion by the sea-shore up close in a movie, and then to actually stand there barefoot in the sand, was to straddle the world of make-believe and reality.

In July 1978, when she got into the IAS, Sivakami was treated by her friends to a trip there. 'Such a vast park and a lot of games and we enjoyed thoroughly. They made me wear a skirt,' recalled Sivakami with a throaty mischievous chuckle. To their disappointment, they did not get to see an actor.

Months later, in one of life's delicious moments, 'When I became the Sub-Collector of Chengalpattu, I was in charge of this whole area. So one day, I had to visit VGP as part of my work. A small cottage was made available where I could have my lunch, do my inspection and leave. I got to meet a famous Tamil actor, and watched him shoot his scenes.'

And in that seemingly casual statement – the facilities of the cottage at her disposal, the easy access to the actor, the flunkeys who would have scurried about ensuring her comfort – lay the immense distance she had travelled, from someone who had once been part of the enthusiastic crowd to an officer who could lord it over people and establishments.

Indeed, the fact that she cleared the much dreaded civil services entrance exam itself serves as inspiration to many. This she owes to her father. 'He was keen to see me as an IAS officer.'

Hot tea was served. 'I am very particular about how it is made.' The tea was perfection itself, not too milky, nor over-boiled, and I sipped slowly trying to make it last.

'Try these snacks,' urged Sivakami hospitably, 'they are different, made of rice flour.'

Sivakami's father, Palanimuthu, was a member of the Legislative Assembly, as an independent candidate. Even though an ex-MLA by the time she was born in 1957, she remembers at least ten or fifteen people calling on him everyday during her childhood. It meant proper behaviour was expected of her at all times.

Her grandmother had the power to heal and villagers would visit her with a sick child, seeking guidance, always with the traditional offering of betel leaves and areca nuts. Sivakami's mother Thandayi had inherited the gift of prophecy or '*arul*' from her mother-in-law when she died.

'We never went to temples. Our family deity is Ponnusamy, very handsome, soldier-like with a big moustache. My father constructed a small temple for him in the fields. I loved the sound of the palm trees shaking and the free flow of wind across the crops. On the dark moon nights of *amavasai*, Father and Mother would fast. They would eat vegetarian food and make offerings to our forefathers. We did not celebrate Deepavali so much as Pongal. That was our main festival, especially Mattu Pongal when cows and bulls are venerated. A priest or *pusari* would come home, and for ten minutes he would shake and sway as he chanted musically.'

When her father joined the Congress, it resulted in the great leader Kamaraj visiting their home. 'I was five or six years old, clinging to my father's hand. Kamaraj lifted me up and asked me my name. He liked my name very much as his mother was called Sivakami. He gave me a handkerchief initialed with a K, which I lost.'

Again Sivakami chuckled, and there was a wonderful, exultant quality to it, conveying the sense of a person who is warm and earthy.

Even though her father was in the Assembly, it did not mean Sivakami grew up in comfort. 'We had lands, that's all. We were too many mouths to be fed. Father married twice, so there were two wives, two grandmothers, thirteen of us.' When he adopted his late sister's children, the size of the family swelled to twenty-two. 'He built a house for which he took loans. We had little resources,' stated Sivakami simply.

That did not deter Palanimuthu from educating his brood. Sivakami was the smartest of her siblings, topping her school. In Holy Cross College, Trichy, she wanted to study Mathematics but 'my father had his own plans. He enrolled me in History, Logic and Advanced English. He had heard that the humanities were preferred for the IAS exam.' In a brief show of independence, Sivakami got her Principal to change her subject to Mathematics but her father did not allow her to actually go through with it.

Sivakami adds, 'I was a good student. I could master anything so I did well in college.' She won a University gold medal in History and stood first in the state in the Tamil language exam which won her two prestigious prizes.

However, 'English was a problem. I could write very well, but I could not speak that well. Later, in Queen Mary's College, I became friendly with a Malaysian who encouraged me to speak in English. Communicating was difficult, even though my pronunciation was good. I acted in English plays and could memorize speeches and deliver them well enough to win a prize, but I struggled to communicate with my limited vocabulary. After joining the IAS, it improved.'

It was around this time that Sivakami discovered the writer in her. 'Our Tamil teacher was a role model for us. Fair, and pretty, and young, she wore a new sari everyday. She was hardly two or three years older than us, and not married. We all vied to win her love and attention. I stood first in class and pleased by my essays she encouraged me to write short stories that she published in the magazine. A story of mine won a prize and then I immersed myself in reading and writing. I loved literature ... the IAS was a secondary thing. I had never seen a collector, never been near the corridors of power.

But when I finished my MA, my father said, "Write the IAS exam."'

It was clear as Sivakami spoke how great an influence her father was in her life, both supportive and authoritative. In order to help her further, he approached an IAS officer whose father he knew, seeking guidance for Sivakami in how best to prepare for the exam. 'The officer was very discouraging. He gave me unachievable targets. He said "It's very tough, be serious, you have to study for fourteen hours a day…" and seemed sceptical that I would ever get through.'

He had not understood Sivakami's grit and true nature. 'I took him at his word and was not at all discouraged. Fourteen hours? I took it as fifteen hours, that's all. I planned my time carefully, figured out how to spend each hour without falling asleep.' Again the rich chuckle.

Sivakami passed the exams. 'It seemed so natural … like taking the next step in my life.' Understandably, her father was thrilled. It was only on joining the service that Sivakami was to learn how big an achievement it truly was. Even among her siblings, only one could get into fruitful service. 'After I got into the IAS, my brother was inspired by me to join the IPS.'

Now an IAS officer herself, albeit a junior one, Sivakami called on the man who had scoffed at her self-belief. 'When I joined he was the Commissioner. I went to make a courtesy call, he did not allow me to come in. He told his secretary, "Ask her to ring up, make an appointment and then come." It took me two years to get an appointment. But there were others who were nice…'

As one of the few women in the service, it took Sivakami some time to understand how the system works. 'There are a lot of political motivations. Access to the better posts or training programmes is limited, if you have no godfathers. There was one particular scholarship programme that every officer went on and I assumed I would go too because I was so hard working. But it did not happen. When I checked, HRD said that because I had not attended a certain domestic training programme,' due to her being pregnant at the time, 'I was blacklisted for the scholarship. By the time I got the remark removed from my file and then finally got the scholarship it was of a much shorter duration.'

Very early in her career, Sivakami realized the importance of her position while interacting with people who came to her with their problems. She had the power to make a difference in their lives.

'I never felt overworked. I loved my work, files after files, meeting after meeting, visit after visit. I knew that because of my orders people were benefitting. I used to be prompt and do everything fast. People still come and tell me, "You dealt with the file so quickly and passed the order, we have never seen an officer like you." A renowned consumer activist, Sundara Mani, said I was sharp as a green chilli!'

One particularly satisfying day involved the Irulas, traditionally a snake-catching tribe, in Villupuram. 'They were not getting the ST caste certificate. Deserving candidates were told, "You are not catching snakes anymore."' When Sivakami was apprised of the problem, she told the District Collector that if he did not make enquiries, she would go there herself to ensure that the certificate was given. In the end, 'I camped at Melmalayanur. The Collector and the RDO and the DRDO, they all came there. The certificate was given in the village. For the Irulas it was such a big thing. Justice should not be delayed.'

Women, especially, sought her help. 'A woman would come saying, "Someone is blocking access to my field, I can't reach it." I would inform her at once when I would be able to inspect her land, and either I would solve the problem or fix another date for the hearing. Often, I gave fruit trees to all the women's groups, to plant in their backyards.'

Sivakami soon realized that a lot of the money meant for Dalit uplift under the Special Component Plan was not reaching the Dalits. 'The money was allocated to various departments. The departments would say they had spent the money but they maintained no records. If you say it was spent on agriculture ... the Dalits are landless ... how can they benefit from agriculture?' So began an attempt to sensitize bureaucrats towards the particular requirements of the SC/ST. 'Activists took class for them during my tenure, with the approval of the Chief Minister.'

Sivakami assumed charge of the Tamil Nadu Tourism Development Corporation and was dismayed by its dollar-earnings which were much below the state's potential for revenue from tourists. 'I went to South Africa, where there are many people of Tamil origin, with my finance manager, and advertised various packages. About twelve packages of sixty members each got sold because it was a good package, but I did not have air-conditioned accommodation for all those people! When I returned I held a board meeting where I had to ask for all those ACs to be fitted in time. Within that year itself, 1993, I had made $100,000. The Joint Secretary was so impressed he wrote to all the tourism boards across India about making it a model for other states.'

When Sivakami held the post of Joint Secretary, Protocol, 'It gave my career a lift. I was the first lady officer to get it. Senior officers would wait in my room, thinking I was close to the Chief Secretary! It was a nice post.'

Her initiative was recognized when she was posted to Tokyo for three years as the Regional Director, East Asia, in charge of thirteen countries. Each month, she visited two of those countries as the sole representative of India. In that period, the tourist inflow from Japan alone almost doubled. 'It also helped me personally, as I earned more.'

By virtue of being a lady officer, Sivakami found that 'Someone else designed your career and you sailed along. Lady officers would always get social welfare, health, and were not given plum posts. I did not get a prime district though some lady officers did manage to get good posts. Sometimes I felt I did not have adequate knowledge of the subject, or my views were not accepted. But I did not feel any particular discrimination. You see, when you held official meetings it was not ladies versus men. It was usually about a technical specialist versus us generalists. When you did not know enough you had to leave it to the experts. Overall, the post carries you.'

However, in being a woman, some things haven't changed. 'One has to be careful while going out alone.' Referring to the beach, just a kilometre away, she said, 'We can't sit there till late or frequent certain spots. Depending on the time, the trouble will be different. Mornings ... a chap will attend to nature's call in front of you. In the afternoon, if you sit in the shade of a boat, they say filthy things as they pass. Evenings ... worse, they act smart.'

Sivakami recounted an amusing incident that occurred when two of her friends came over to stay. 'The three of us went for a walk past 11 p.m. at the Palavakkam beach, where people know me. We saw a man sitting all alone and asked him, "Are you not afraid?" He replied, "First I was, but I know her," pointing to me, "so then I relaxed. When she comes everyone is scared because she can beat up two or three men." I was so happy. It gave me confidence.'

We smiled at each other.

Being a woman *and* Dalit had other drawbacks at the professional level. 'If there is no political will, a file will not be cleared. The way it works is on the basis of caste. There were four or five Brahmin officers whose files were always cleared. If *I* sent one, they would have a thousand queries.'

Getting the state government to release centrally allotted funds was particularly difficult. 'Rs 100 crores were set aside for tribals, but not released. First, they said they had to find the land. Then it was the year end and so on, it kept getting postponed. Then I heard that the money was actually being used for some other expenditure.

'When I came to be posted to the Adi Dravidar Welfare Department, I saw the true face and spirit of the government towards poor people. It is like taking from the belly of the poor or eating a scavenger's money. I felt that if the state was not helping them financially, the least they could do was allow the Government of India to do so. No one seems to care about the common man so I thought, *Time is up for me.*'

The feeling was prescient because very soon Sivakami was transferred – to what is called a 'punishment' posting, lacking in scope and importance. 'The moment they understood that I knew about them, they gave me the sort of post where you idle and draw a salary. But I refused to get punished ... I used to find time to write.'

Sivakami is widely known as the author of the first novel by a Tamil Dalit woman, written in 1989, and translated by herself in English as *The Grip of Change*.

Gowri, one of the main characters in *The Grip of Change*, and her father Kathamuthu, reflect Sivakami and her own father Palanimuthu in many ways. Sivakami describes caste interactions as they unfold in a small village in Tamil Nadu and the change that begins when a younger generation comes to the fore, with new ideas. She writes, *The novel* The Grip of Change *is a process of understanding the dynamics of caste and the "woman" who was inextricably involved in the process.*

In her novel, she observes that *Even among the lower castes, hierarchies existed ... Similar to almost all other human communities, the women were considered to be lower than men. Everyone established their worth by pointing to those beneath them.*

A feminist, Sivakami explores the tensions in a home where two women have to share a man, and also put up with other women who may attract his eye. While in real life it could not have been pleasant, Sivakami adds a touch of humour to her description.

Ten years after *The Grip of Change*, Sivakami wrote another book *Gowri: Author's Notes*, where she reflected on the intangible connections between reality and fiction in the author's subconscious, between events that have actually taken place and the solutions a novel can offer. '*She wanted to prove that there was no such thing as the full and complete truth.*'

In this self-critique of her first novel, there are several moving passages. One about her father Palanimuthu:

When her father was elected a member of the legislative assembly in the first general elections, the tahsildar had not offered him a seat when he had entered the man's office. The tahsildar had also insulted her father in the manner in which he had addressed him. After her father left, the tahsildar had apparently grumbled about being forced to treat a Parayan as an equal.

Her father had come home, locked himself in a room and wept.

And one about the young Sivakami:

Why had she longed for good clothes and good food?
The education inspector was to pay a visit to her school.

She wore a faded blue dhavani. She wore it every day,
even on holidays when she had to work in the plantain
grove or gather firewood. It had a few holes. But she wore
it neatly, hiding them within the folds. However, the
headmistress possessed eagle eyes. "Don't you have another
dhavani? You are the school pupil leader! Borrow a dhavani
from someone else. Shenbaga, you have many clothes. Take
her home and give her a dhavani. Quick."

They walked in uneasy silence. Shenbaga's father,
a Nadar who owned a shop that sold kitchen utensils,
stopped her at the gate. Shenbaga went inside and came out
immediately. "My mother says we can't lend you a dhavani.
You belong to the Parayan caste ... What shall we do?"

Sivakami talked about her official work and her writing. 'The more the pressure ... it is necessary to express yourself, to write. My creativity comes from my work. I have had rich experiences, meeting different people ... I owe that to the IAS. A poor girl generally is not given much opportunity. What experiences would she have? But I got a vast canvas. My heroine is different from me, born out of me but a different piece.' And again Sivakami chuckled, a ripple of silver. And I thought of a line she had written: *Nothing in the novel was untrue. But the novel was false, she felt.*

While the writer in her came to the fore, it bothered her that she 'could not do full justice to the work'. Sivakami resigned from the service in 2008. 'When I was in my own world of career and achievement, my eyes were on that. Now they are opened. I thought I should do something with my experience and knowledge. Let me play my role. Whether people support me or not is a different story.'

She joined the Bahujan Samaj Party and contested the Lok Sabha poll from Kanyakumari where she got about 7,000 votes.

In 2009, she formed her own party Samuga Samuthuva Padai after Ambedkar's Samata Sainik Dal. 'My father was basically a Congress person, so Ambedkar had not reached him. Father knew about him, but he could not read him because of the language barrier. That is, while Ambedkar *manrams* – gatherings of Ambedkar's followers – were there, Dr Ambedkar's writings had not been translated. The northern belt of Tamil Nadu had a greater awareness of him. Perambalur was in central Tamil Nadu ... as a child, I had not read about him in my textbooks. But when I became the Collector of Tuticorin, I read his books for the Ambedkar Centenary celebrations.'

My eyes drifted to the portraits on the wall: Ambedkar and Buddha side by side. 'I offer flowers to Buddha,' said Sivakami. 'I am attracted to him and try to follow him. I don't go to temples and I don't spend much time exploring the existence of God. Instead, I believe that love is God, and I try everyday to love people, nature, all living beings and not abuse anyone. That is the best way of worship.'

Inspired by Ambedkar, she talked about her effort to bring change. 'I may not succeed, but that does not mean I should not try. One needs to have a good disciplined cadre. I have at least a hundred people who can work with me and ten thousand members.'

Sivakami wants to help as many women as she can. 'I had initiated a lot of things such as mobilizing 2.5 lakh women. Though replicated by the Government, my work will not be acknowledged. Afterwards J Jayalalithaa started her young women camps and M Karunanidhi started the women's conference. Similarly, I had the idea of a Dalit land rights movement. I made someone the leader and mobilized lakhs and lakhs of people. Later, Karunanidhi announced two acres of free land to the poor. He gave but not to the people who needed it.'

Sivakami firmly believes that 'those not directly engaged in agriculture should not own it.' From being seen as mere property it should be seen as the source of livelihood that it is. She is against absentee landlords – 'land needs soul and heart.' If those who cultivate the land own it, 'then there will be removal of poverty because 60 per cent of landless agriculturists are Dalits.' But that goes directly against the interests of the landowners who 'dominate in assembly and Parliament'.

If schools were built in Dalit localities, 'it would change the atmosphere … children going to school, teachers taking classes. It dissipates violence and fewer men would go to toddy shops.' Also, 'every village should have playgrounds for women. When women come out to play, give expression to their body, then their courage comes to the fore.' She also believes there should be work sheds for women where they can work on handmade crafts, say palm-leaf baskets, mats or fans, and the place would serve as a community centre and crèche for their children. 'It would help create political awareness.'

By working on land related issues and the proper implementation of reservation, Sivakami hopes to empower women in the villages. 'People should not be wanting to move to cities. By giving them land, even if it is almost barren, they could grow small crops like greens and fruit-bearing trees like papaya and drumstick.'

On the whole however, reservation has certainly helped. 'Of course, we have come up because of it. But it is not a be-all and end-all. The rich among the Backward Castes get the benefits, the rest have only the pride of being BC without the benefit. There should be a proportionate sharing of resources. Dhobis, fishermen, barbers, for example, are not reaping the benefits of reservation.'

Did she see a revolution taking place as it did in Russia? No. 'The communist parties are captured by the petit bourgeois. Also, our belief system encourages this notion that it is our fate to be born this way and live in poverty – the karma theory. You accept your inability and don't want to try anything.'

Sivakami drew a deep breath. '*I* try. Let me fail but I will not give up. Maybe the younger generation will take it up. Our generation, we can talk across the table as equals. Maybe the next generation will want to share. We are not like our forefathers but progress is not automatic. We have to work towards it.'

Does she miss the heady rush of the power of government office?

'I should have resigned much earlier, but my children were young, I was building a house, and a career. Now, I am happy with my activism.'

Free of the proprieties demanded by high office, in her spare time the writer in Sivakami is content 'eating groundnuts at the local bus stop, watching people go by. Sometimes, I may visit the tea stall nearby. This freedom is not there in the village.'

It is as a writer perhaps that Sivakami wields even greater power. If for centuries Dalits had no access to education, and the written word, it also meant their voice did not form part of the canon of Indian regional literature. But now there is a significant body of work, both in the original language across the regions as well as translated into English, and it is in adding the Dalit experience to the record of life as imagined and lived in different parts of India, that Sivakami, writing in Tamil, has made a lasting mark.

3

Coping with Change

'I am a city boy … I can't think of leaving Chennai.'
Saravana Sakthivale

Every morning, dutifully, Saravana Sakthivale performs a pleasurable rite in the private space of his bathroom. Uncapping a small tin cylinder, he takes a good pinch of the pale brown powder inside and conveying it to his nostril, inhales briskly. Almost immediately, his eyes start to water, and he braces himself for the peppery hit. Earlier, he would sneeze, but now his nose is accustomed to this daily assault. By the time he has finished bathing, a thick brown mucus is flowing out of it. For the next half an hour, as he emerges freshly dressed, there's a pleasant buzz in his head.

Saravana, a friend of mine, inherited a century-old snuff making company about twenty years ago. Since then the industry has been so affected by tax and other legislation against its use, that his profits have plummeted. Here is a case where changing fortunes might mean Saravana can no longer carry on family tradition, despite wanting to. Should he continue, or should he close the business? For genial, good natured Saravana, it is a 'daily dilemma'. Several hits of snuff a day help; after all he must test his product.

I would have to head north-west to Kilpauk, one of the oldest localities, cutting across central Chennai to reach his house. Due to the increased traffic, diversions required by the on-going Metro project, and the distance, this is an area I rarely visit. I decided to take an auto. Soon, I was rattling across the city, half-listening to the talkative driver as I looked out at the view.

And so, over the Adyar bridge, turning left on Greenways Road, through Alwarpet, approaching the central crossroads at Gemini Circle, on to the long Nungambakkam High Road, then right all the way to Ega theatre and left down Poonamallee. Though the roads and streets remain fixed – the underlying geography of the place – their names can change, the house numbers change, and everyday there is a flux of people and vehicles that make the place ever-changing, ever-the-same.

The eye sees everything, absorbs the stream of life, most of which is similar day after day, but also registers minute changes or interesting details – the *potti kadai* or shack selling tea and snacks that one never visited but has vanished overnight; a man steering his engine-fitted cart as though it were a chariot; rose petals crushed crimson on the road indicating a corpse has taken its last journey; a labourer bent double under the weight of a sack of rice, his sun-burnt torso covered in sweat; a dashing policeman on a sturdy Bullet.

I was passing an area that actually had pavements; wide enough for a family to build a little shelter of plastic sheeting and live there. Children dressed in rags, their hair like straw, played on the hot cement. A little boy wore only a shirt with no buttons. His stomach bulged out and his legs were like sticks. That hungry child played with a ball, surrounded by noise and rolling wheels, dust and the stench of the gutter nearby. But even there, the mother had carefully spread a tattered mat for her baby and covered its sleeping form with a bit of patched cloth.

To live in any big city in India is to see these sights everyday and be assaulted by an enormous sense of helplessness, to live without being able to express that terrible feeling. It converts itself into a keen appreciation of the inequalities of life, a sense of gratitude for what one had been given.

It wasn't so long ago that cattle and goats also shared the roads, and cowdung was gathered with care, slapped on walls for fuel cakes. Filling umpteen pots of water for domestic use, earning enough to buy rice for the day's meals, industry and labour unceasing, debts taken for marriages and deaths, illness and school fees, it is a harsh life for most in the city. A rupee, devalued though it is, is still hard to earn.

The landscape – part urban, part incredibly rural – comes into being each day with light, and vanishes at night when the streets empty, people retreating to their spaces private or otherwise, only to spill onto the roads with renewed determination the next day.

When Saravana was newly married, his wife Malar pleaded with him, 'Please stop using snuff.' He told her, gently but firmly, 'I don't drink, I don't smoke. I have no bad habits. This is my work, *our* bread and butter, so don't interfere in this.'

It was not a good time to have asked him anyway. Saravana's father NVSP Shunmuga Vale had passed away days before the wedding in June 1996. 'It still bothers me when I think of my last fight with him … it was over the design of my wedding invitation. "I have conducted nine weddings," he thundered. I had retorted, "This is my first experience!"' Since all preparations had been made, and the invitations sent out by Shunmuga Vale, the family decided to go ahead with the ceremony, as though he were indeed present there. Overnight almost, Saravana found himself married, the head of his father's snuff factory NV Shunmugam and Co, and at age thirty, the inheritor of his debts. 'I was in a daze.'

A stream of dealers and employees came calling. They were worried. 'Don't shut down the business,' they pleaded. 'Our livelihoods depend on you. Do not let us down.' They invoked patriarchy of a different kind; the factory-owner as a father figure, godfather even, never mind that he was younger than them. It moved Saravana. 'I told them not to worry.'

His brother had already set up his own leather business, so of the two of them it would be up to Saravana to run the snuff factory. Until then, he had helped his father in various aspects of the business, purchasing tobacco leaves, the actual process of making snuff, and selling it across Tamil Nadu, but he had never been involved in the finances. Those reins were firmly held by his father.

When Saravana took a look at the numbers, and it took him over a year to properly grasp their implications, he was dismayed. He had inherited debts of a crushing magnitude. Interest on interest on interest had tripled the original amount at one bank. Vendors and business associates claimed they had given soft loans but had no paperwork to prove it. It was a matter of honour; by clearing even those dubious ones, Saravana would uphold his father's name. That was paramount.

His brother and he spent many an hour trying to figure a way out of the mess. They prayed to the deity at Palani, after whom they were named, to keep them going. At other times, they remembered wistfully the golden history of their family enterprise.

The company was established in 1904, by their great-grandfather Nagoor Velayudham Shunmugam. Of the Nadar trader community, he had the sharp instinct for business and sensed opportunity in 'Patnam' or the great city of Madras. Leaving his village Nagoor, he moved to Madras. Preparing his snuff with care – its aroma reminiscent of mangoes – he carried it on his head from door to door. Soon, he had regular customers, addicted to his '*vellai podi*' or 'white' snuff, a finer variety than the 'black' powder made of ground tobacco.

Shunmugam had two sons, Palani Vale Nadar, Saravana's grandfather and Muruga Vale Nadar. The period when they inherited the business and ran it well coincided with a golden period in the sales of snuff. They had a huge factory, spread over an acre of land at Tondiarpet, an old manufacturing locality in the north of the city, and up until his death at an early age in 1948, Palani Vale Nadar rode a horse to work every morning. 'They sold a lot of snuff. The people who used it were a low class of people, the masses. They could not afford cigarettes, so they smoked beedis or inhaled snuff.'

The use of snuff is a ubiquitous private act carried out in public. There is a typical, furtive, gesture made by someone using it, be it gardener, handyman or labourer: left hand shielding the nose, the snuff inhaled off the right index figure with a dramatic sniff. A user of snuff can be identified anywhere by the discoloured digits of his right hand, the wipe-stains on his lungi or yellowing veshti, and a peculiar, disagreeable odour that emanates from him. A bus driver might climb into his seat and use it just before he starts his engine, to chase away post-lunch stupor. A watchman might use it to counter the December chill.

Just as women chew tobacco rather than smoke it, many of them prefer coating their teeth with the black variety of snuff, allowing the nicotine to seep in through their gums – a use it was not designed for.

Saravana's father was eleven when his father passed away, too young to participate in the business; his uncle continued to run it. As soon as he turned eighteen, Shunmuga Vale entered the business. Having lost his mother too, he ended up having to take care of his family, arranging to educate his brothers and sisters.

Through the fifties and sixties, as the snuff business flourished, the family's income grew enormously. Calendars to be distributed to their agents and customers, were printed in Germany with a modern but stylized rendition of Krishna or other mythological characters, and are now collector's items.

All of a sudden, there were problems on the partnership front. His uncle had five sons, and there were many disputes over the running of the company until Shunmuga Vale decided to buy out his uncle's share. At the time, the Rs 5 or 6 lakhs he paid was a substantial sum of money. Soon his brother joined the company and they ran it together until 1983.

It was perhaps a sign of the times, whereas the earlier generation of brothers had managed amicably, Shunmuga Vale and his brother had a falling out. Other people with vested interests fermented the trouble and the company was divided. The brothers agreed to retain the trade name, an asset they did not want to tamper with, but split their territory area-wise. There was a certain finality to it – even the manufacturing of the very same product would be duplicated by each brother; a wall was built in the factory dividing it in halves.

Saravana finished school at Don Bosco in 1985; his father wanted him to join the business at once but had to wait another three years. At his mother's insistence, Saravana studied Economics in Loyola College. When the lectures dragged on, Saravana was in popular demand for the little tin of snuff he carried. If the lecturers wondered why students sneezed a lot in the afternoons, they never caught on. Several of his friends swear they made it through college thanks to the perk-me-up it provided.

The city of Chennai was expanding, and pollution increased with the growth of industry. Newly conscious of the effects of pollution, people in the neighbourhood of the factory in Tondiarpet complained about the fumes spewed into the city air. In 1992, Shunmuga Vale moved his factory to Poonamallee, quite some distance into the outskirts. The snuff industry was still extremely profitable and father and son Saravana worked together until the fateful day in 1996.

Now, feeling the tremendous weight of debts, Saravana was trying to figure out how to repay a bank loan where the interest alone had accumulated to more than Rs 10 lakhs. By the time the issue was taken up by the Debt Recovery Tribunal, it had added up to Rs 16 lakhs. But even in the grim situation there was always room for simple human kindness. 'My brother and I, we went to see the zonal manager of the bank, a very nice elderly man, like a father to us. I was explaining to him how I was in no position to pay back the entire amount. Just then a clerk came up and told us derisively, "Do you know how much your dues are today? Rs 16 lakhs when your original borrowing was only Rs 3.5 lakhs." The manager said to him, "Shut up. I am talking to them." He helped us settle the loan for much less.'

In the year 1997, there was an unexpected and huge dip in sales, and Saravana was anxious. 'I could not understand why, but continued to maintain quality and the next year it picked up.' It took Saravana more than five years to pay off all the debts. Throughout, he was lucky to have his brother's help, 'He is still legally involved though he is happy with his leather business. We used to live together. So every morning, we would discuss how to tackle the problems.'

Meanwhile another crisis erupted. The regular suppliers of raw material, who had flourished due to the company, stopped supplying from Andhra Pradesh. 'The soil and water there are perfect for tobacco ... the tobacco for snuff is different from that for cigarettes. It takes two kilos of tobacco to make a kilo of snuff. After the leaves are plucked and dried, it takes eight days to process them with jaggery and water. Then they send it to us in bundles.' Saravana had to assure them that come what may he would repay them regularly, before they resumed trade.

But the biggest crisis, which began around the year 2000, was something unforeseen, and it had to do with changing times and the snuff business itself, linked as it is to tobacco. It gnawed at Saravana's peace everyday – how long would he be able to run his more than hundred-year-old company profitably?

An astronomical burden of taxes had fallen on his profit margins, flattening them with each passing budget. The taxes really were aimed at the organized sector of the tobacco industry, cigarette manufacturers, but they also affected businessmen like Saravana, whose scale of production and area of operation were much smaller. 'There is no way we can fight, we need the might of the cigarette guys to fight. The government is not totally banning cigarettes because they bring in money. They've banned gutkha and paan masala … linked to oral cancer. So snuff might go too even though the nicotine content is lower compared to cigarettes!'

To add to his woes, the market for snuff was shrinking rapidly. 'Each time a customer dies, my village retailers who know each customer personally, feel sad.' As the older customers died, they were not replaced by the younger generation – snuff was passé; beedis and gutka were in. 'In those days they would hide and put snuff, now they feel very shy to use snuff. But gutka can be put in the mouth openly … and beedis and cigarettes, you can take a puff and hide in your palm.' Saravana increasingly needed several whiffs of snuff a day to revive his spirits.

And it was to look at the way snuff is manufactured that Saravana and Malar and I set off from his home near the sprawling Kilpauk Water Works, from where in 1914, the water treatment and supply to the city was systematized, to visit his factory.

As we passed Anna Nagar, an area just beginning to be developed when my parents moved to Madras in the sixties, it was possible to see how the city had extended far past earlier boundaries, and connected by better roads, places once considered outside the city were now legitimately linked to it, embraced even.

Indeed it was this outward expansion, in waves as it were, that was creating difficulties for Saravana. The factory, spread over three large sheds, was on rented premises. Ironically, or tragically even, his forefathers, who had lived in some of the best areas, Spur Tank Road, Harrington Road, College Road – and who imported a Mercedes in 1972 – had not thought to buy land for a home or factory. 'By the time my father put together Rs 3.5 lakhs advance to buy the six-ground property we were living in on Casa Major Road, it had been sold,' rued Saravana. It meant that as rents increased over the years, Saravana had to shift to progressively smaller premises in not-so-posh areas.

But those such as Saravana's landlord, who had invested in land which might not have risen much in value over years, woke one day to find themselves rich. 'Whenever the owner has to get a daughter married, he sells some of the land. The more he sells, my factory area becomes smaller and smaller.'

We drove along a highway flanked by many residential high-rises in various stages of construction, and Saravana pointed one out that was said to have been built on an old graveyard. Turning off the main road onto a gravelly lane, he said, 'We've reached.' All I could see was a newly built showroom displaying sleek bikes. The plate glass windows still bore crude X-s painted in white as warning.

Threading our way down a narrow passage behind the modern showroom, past a low entrance, we were suddenly in old Madras. Three cottage-like structures rose off the ground, single-storied with a low threshold and red-tiled roof. They enclosed a yard whose earth had been swept in honour of my arrival, a yard open to the sky. Tobacco leaves piled to one side, brooms, baskets, tins, other odds and ends, but chiefly the appearance of the men and women working there, added to the rural atmosphere.

Already, the overpoweringly humid smell of snuff had reached me, somewhat disagreeable but familiar, carrying notes of organic rotting, dirt and heated tobacco. In the semi-gloom of the main shed, an elderly woman in a crumpled sari sat peeling the mid-rib off the large sticky-with-jaggery leaf. Near her, a thin woman roasted cut bits of leaf, turning them with care on a large clay vessel placed over glowing coal. In the basic simplicity of their attire – cloth covering body, single bangles of glass, yellow marriage-thread in place of a necklace, the roughness of their work-hardened palms, bare feet, the stoic calmness invested in their manual labour, they represented the million men and women who toiled in the city under difficult working conditions.

And yet they were semi-skilled labourers, and the king among them was a man with greying hair who mixed the snuff powder – a specialist rare to find. I watched him straddle an aluminium tub filled with ground tobacco powder, four different grades of it, and the right proportion of ghee, 'the binding substance' and edible lime and white pepper 'for the hit'. Bending over, he raked the snuff over with his hands, shifting mounds of it in an almost sensuous way but with the deliberation of long practice.

Further inside, two middle-aged men, stripped to their durable inner-shorts, stood roasting the tobacco in a furnace, their skin gleaming with sweat. Here, near the blatant heat of the fire, the fumes were upon me in seconds, searing my skin, burning my eyes, invading my nostrils, choking me. I was barely able to stand there a minute before I ran to the yard seeking fresh air, tears streaming from my eyes; Malar followed soon after. Adjusting to the bright sunlight outside, there was fresh trauma to the eye.

Saravana came out in a while with one of the 'roasting' men, sturdily built, with dry hair and tired eyes, now wearing a blue chequered lungi and hastily buttoning his worn, faded shirt. 'He's the head *maistri*. We have worked together for many years, he's my age. The younger guys are not able to adapt, they can't take the smell. They quit. So it is difficult to find labour for this work. I have to start training them with the minor jobs. They come here, to Kumannan Chavadi, from Tondiarpet,' a distance of more than 25 kms, 'Even though I pay them bus fare, they are very irregular.'

The furnace, the machines for grinding the tobacco in the second shed, packing the snuff, these were all brought in by Saravana's father. Bright golden flecks of sandalpaste and dots of kumkum on each of them spoke of the recent Ayudha puja, when all manner of tools, machines and vehicles across the city are worshipped.

'Earlier, when everything was done by hand, we had about thirty or forty labourers, now I have twelve. We used to crush the tobacco using heavy wooden poles, that gives it a great flavour, and also hand-roast it. But skilled labour is not easily available so we do as much as we can by machines and finish by hand to maintain quality.'

Thick black smoke rose into the afternoon air from a tall metal pipe on the roof. Here too, neighbours had begun to complain.

'The last stage is packing. Snuff has to be dry – the only moisture in it is from the ghee – or it will get stuck inside the nose. Equally, too fine a powder is bad. The right sort of packing is critical. A huge log of wood is used to tightly pack it into big 15 kg tins. The flavour develops over time. Five days later it will be better ... when I go to the market, I'll test it.

'We sell in different packages. The smallest is the 10 gm tin which costs Rs 3. The sachet cost Re 1, and we thrived on those, but I stopped using them after the Supreme Court banned the metallized plastic material as it is not bio-degradable. From every side we get hit, this ban is only on tobacco products. It is okay to sell chips in them but not tobacco!

'Plastic melts in the heat. Paper absorbs moisture, which affects the snuff, so I can't use paper sachets even though there is a demand. In rural areas, the one person handling the shop has no help to decant the tins and make smaller packets. It is easier for him to just tear away the sachet and give.'

As he spoke, my mind conjured the image of a shack or thatched kiosk selling biscuits and boiled sweets in thick glass jars, glasses of hot tea or rose milk perhaps, while sachets of shampoo, supari and snuff dangled like streamers from the roof, stirring whenever the breeze blew.

We then settled ourselves in the third and smallest shed – the office. Malar had carried from home a knotted plastic-wire basket, which many Tamilian women pride themselves on making, stuffed with things. Delving into it, she conjured up plates and cups, and fragrant coffee and an assortment of snacks. Soon, we had an impromptu picnic spread across Saravana's desk.

I crunched on a ball of groundnuts-in-jaggery, and Saravana continued to talk about snuff-making and his dilemmas. When he took over the company in 1996, he sold 1,200 kilos of snuff a week. His sales were mainly in Thirunelveli, in the deep South, spreading across the small towns and villages beyond Madurai where he had a depot. The excise duty was around 20 to 23 per cent.

'My sales figures were increasing, and thanks to that I was able to pay off my debts. Then, from 2000 onwards, taxes just jumped 20, 30, 40, 50, 60, and stabilized at 76 per cent, later a cess was added so it became 79 per cent! My sales kept dropping. In the last seven years, my sales have dropped by 50 per cent.'

The latest addition to his woes was the VAT or value added tax, which came in 2011. 'I have to pay 20 per cent VAT but that is not a simple calculation. If you take a base of Rs 100 and add Rs 80 as taxes, then the VAT is 20 per cent of that, or 36 per cent. If in one year alone there is a increase of 36 per cent, how can you manage?'

Today, because snuff is a tobacco product, he pays 115 per cent as taxes. His sense of humour intact, Saravana rattled off the list of taxes, 'Income tax, central excise tax, sales tax, service tax, professional tax, value added tax. All we need is a birth and death tax! It is crippling.'

Doubly affected by rising cost prices and taxes, Saravana's profit margins have taken a hit. 'Earlier, I would gross 40 per cent and make a net profit of about 10 to 15 per cent. Now on Rs 215 I am earning Rs 20, a gross of only ten percent. *And*, sales are falling.'

Of about as many as 125 companies selling snuff, Saravana has seen many of the big names – all a jumble of letters … the founder's initials – decline over the past decade. 'A lot of the big companies have collapsed. They were doing very well … but it is a tough market now.' Another family-owned company split into two. 'The two factions were at war. Let's say the cost of making snuff was Rs 45 a kg. One would sell it at Rs 50, then the other fellow would sell at Rs 48. Immediately the first chap would price it at Rs 46. They wiped each other out by underselling.' Small retailers who benefited eagerly asked Saravana what 'special' rate he would offer them. 'I said, "Mine is Rs 50 for everyone. Want to buy … buy."'

When taxes are this high, explained Saravana, the benefits of evading them are enormous. 'If you avoid paying it you can pass it on to your customers. It is very difficult to do this business honestly. We who pay taxes cannot survive.'

Several new companies have popped up on the scene, lured by the possibility of illegitimate gains. 'They are thriving ... blooming. Let's say I sell for Rs 200, they will sell their snuff at Rs 130, without a bill. The retailer is very happy, and will pass on some of his benefit to the customer. The new ones succeed because of underselling, tax evasion and using inferior quality tobacco. We have become very small, whereas two of the new companies have become big in this way.'

Saravana referred to the brand name NVS Snuff, and what it stands for. 'We are a very old company; Father said we will not bend to anyone. We are selling today because of the quality or we would have been finished five, six years ago. Our retailers have been loyal. Even though business is dropping, they have a lot of respect for us. There are about forty families dependent on me. But now I don't know how long we will run.'

Could he not explore markets in other states? 'The biggest market is in West Bengal. I get a lot of orders from Calcutta, but they want it without bills!' Saravana stated his position clearly, 'I may not able to have a lavish lifestyle but I can keep afloat. I have cleared all my liabilities and kept my father's name. I don't have my own house, nor my own factory but I sleep properly at night.'

Indeed, not owning land on which to build a factory has caused Saravana the necessity of having to relocate. 'I need to find a place where there are no homes, nor schools nearby. I had rented premises in Red Hills but the people nearby did not want a snuff factory there. I kept the shed for six months without using it. Then I discovered that electricity bills are very low in the area, no business is flourishing there … it's not lucky. So I'm still searching for a place.'

Given the importance of Madurai in his distribution network, and the difficulty in sourcing labourers in Chennai, wouldn't it solve all his problems simultaneously if he moved his factory to Madurai? 'It would be much easier to produce from there … my uncle's son did just that. But I am a city boy and the amenities are better here, including schools for my children. I can't think of leaving Chennai.'

4

Inheriting History

'We were ruling much of South India, the area called Carnatic.'
Nawab Mohammed Abdul Ali,
The Eighth Prince of Arcot

Central to the story of the expanding city of Madras is the noun Arcot, both as the name of a place and the title of a ruler. So important was Arcot to the story of the British consolidating their power from Fort St. George, that when the first railway station of south India was opened in Madras, in 1856, the train ran from Royapuram to Arcot.

A living link to the Nawabs of the Carnatic and their encounters with the British, and the French, the Prince of Arcot contributes to the sense of continuity in the city. Interestingly, the Arcots are still given the privilege of being addressed by their title, though other Indian royalty lost their privy purses and attendant privileges in 1971.

I set off to meet His Highness the Prince of Arcot, Al-Hajj Nawab Ghulam Mohammad Abdul Ali Khan Bahadur, history personified.

Down the Ramakrishna Mutt Road, heading towards the temple tank at Mylapore, I realized that much of the land I was driving across once belonged to the Nawabs of Arcot, the Prince's ancestors. Indeed, the Nawab Wallajah's gift of land in Mylapore to the Kapaleeshwarar temple resulted in the vast tank. The tapering gopuram tower of the Mylapore temple, the cluster of coconut trees around, and the steps leading down to the waters of the tank is a composite, abiding image of the city, and its existence a testimony to Hindu-Muslim amity.

Now heading into congested Triplicane, I was in one of the oldest parts of the city, dominated by the Wallajah 'Big' mosque and the ancient Parthasarathy temple. Given the 300-odd 'mansions' crammed into narrow streets, with dingy rooms to let for single men, it is also an area with a high density of bachelors. An entire microcosm – eateries, *kaiyendi-bhavans* or mobile carts, pavement food-vendors, juice stalls, messes specializing in regional cooking, fruit sellers, dhobis, internet cafes and tea shops – exists to meet their needs.

Amir Mahal, the Arcot palace, lies between the arterial Mount Road, and the bustling locality of Triplicane.

Wanting my teenaged son to see the palace as well, I had brought him along. Passing beneath an imposing gateway, I saw an array of sleek black cannons on wheels before I reached the main building, recently renovated, its exterior a deep brick red and yellow.

The walls of the long main hall, and its high raftered ceiling, were painted a cool off-white edged with gilt. Heavy rosewood furniture, covered in brocade was arranged in a series of suites on both sides. At my feet, a red carpet blazed down the centre, past the ionic columns, old palanquins, canopied witness boxes, and ran up a wide wooden staircase at the far end.

Soon we were ushered into the Prince's office-room, a recorded blessing in Arabic floating down on our heads as the door opened before us. Well-built, in his sixties, the Prince is extremely affable, his grey beard lending him the air of a wise statesman. A striking photo on the wall, of a much younger Prince with Rajiv Gandhi showed him in a different, more handsome, light; the two men looked remarkably similar.

Following my gaze, the Prince commented, 'He visited Amir Mahal. It was taken one month and two days before he died.'

Attendants were summoned and sent scurrying to fetch refreshments. While we waited, the Prince traced the story of his ancestors, the Nawabs and Princes of Arcot, and their connection with Madras.

'We were ruling much of south India, the area called Carnatic. Emperor Aurangzeb bestowed the title Nawab of the Carnatic on Zulfikar Ali who won the Fort of Gingee in 1698,' deep in the southern peninsula. Most of that vast area, spreading across what today is Andhra Pradesh, Karnataka and of course Tamil Nadu, was part of the Mughal empire. Confirming the grant of Madras, Zulfikar Ali gave the British the grant of three villages Egmore, Purasawalkam and Tondiarpet, while Triplicane was by this time theirs. His successor was even more munificent, giving the British five: Tiruvottiyur, Nungambakkam, Vyasarpady, Kathiwakkam and Sathangudi.

The third Nawab, Saadatullah, tried to undo this generosity. He wanted all five villages back and then the earlier three as well. After negotiations, the earlier grants were ratified. It was in his time, after the death of Aurangzeb, that the title of Nawab became hereditary and the court moved to Arcot, by the river Palar. In the time of the sixth Nawab, Muhammad, Saiyid, murdered young, the British obtained five more villages of Perambur, Ernavore, Sadiankuppam, Pudubakkam and Vepery in 1742.

'Since he died while still young, his dynasty came to an end. His uncle Muhammad Anwaruddin, born in Hardoi in Uttar Pradesh, became the seventh Nawab. He was a direct descendant of the Second Caliph. He was almost eighty when the seventh Nawab fought against Chanda Sahib who had allied with the French, in the Battle of Ambur and he died on the battlefield.'

Imagining the din and gore of battle, of dying the ultimate warrior's death, of a line of ancestors who charged bravely into war and belatedly registering the pistols hung on the wall of the room, I asked the Nawab, 'Are you trained in how to use a gun?'

He chuckled at the thought. 'No! I don't know how to fire a gun. No shikar either.' The Nawab had studied in a convent school Church Park (which later became exclusively for girls), before completing his studies at Madras Christian College school.

Trays were brought in, fine crockery piled with food: sandwiches made of freshly baked bread, biscuits from Dubai, sweets and stewed apricot or *khubani ka meetha*. And steaming tea.

'Have, have,' the Prince ensured that all the snacks were served, his manner genuinely hospitable. For a while we might have been in Lucknow, following the formal niceties of *'pehle aap'*.

He returned to the subject of his ancestors. 'The most celebrated of the Nawabs was Mohammad Ali Wallajah, the eighth Nawab. In 1765, he became the sovereign ruler of the Carnatic, backed by the British. He decided to move from Arcot to Madras and wanted to build a palace inside Fort St. George. But the British chose Chepauk to the south of the fort as the site, close enough that they could defend it.'

The Nawab set about building a grand palace. It was most probably Paul Benfield, variously company servant, financier, architect who both designed and built it for him. He also fuelled the Nawab's extravagance in ways that benefited Benfield, his principal creditor.

Nawab Wallajah, needing larger and larger sums to maintain his army, his court retinue, to fund the wars involving the British waged on his territories and against Maratha strongholds such as Tanjore, borrowed against the revenues from his domains and soon Benfield was not his only creditor.

What otherwise might have been a simple matter between borrower and lender, became an enormous debt the size of the Carnatic. The 'Carnatic debts' were the subject of debate in the British Parliament and among the British merchants and company servants in Madras there was an 'Arcot interest' whose riches were contingent on the Nawab's ballooning state of debt.

The sprawling Chepauk palace built by Nawab Wallajah was an impressive addition to the skyline of Madras, when viewed from the sea. With its minarets and arches it combined in itself elements of Islamic and regional Hindu architecture in what would later be called the Indo Saracenic style. Apart from the residential quarters at Khalas Mahal and Humayun Mahal, there were gardens, bathing pavilions, elephant and horse stables spread over a 117 acres.

While the Nawab gave priceless diamonds as gifts, such as the Arcot diamonds and the Pigot diamond, he also donated generously to charitable and religious causes. In Mecca, he made arrangements for pilgrims. 'He sent people from Madras to purchase the lands and to put up a shelter. At one time there were more than five hundred *rubats*' or shelters for pilgrims, 'of Indian origin, now only four are left. Of those one is ours, and still in my control. The original waqf building was there for two hundred or more years till 1986. When the Saudi authorities acquired a lot of properties near the Holy Kaaba including ours, they gave us compensation, so we purchased a new seven-storey building which accommodates 160 pilgrims. You know, the *nazirs* who went there as caretakers in Nawab Wallajah's time ... the *same* family continues to look after it.'

The Prince spoke of Nawab Wallajah's many acts that helped not only Muslim pilgrims but Hindus and Christians as well. 'During his forty-six years of rule, he donated lots of land to Hindu temples in many places such as Kanchipuram and Srirangapatnam. He donated the land where later St Joseph's College and Bishop Heber College came up in Trichy. We are talking of secularism today, he practised it then. He was great no doubt.'

And when he gave land to the Kapaleeshwarar temple, 'he requested them to let Muslims use the tank for Muharram. These rituals are not part of orthodox Islam ... they carry *panjas*. To this day, the officials of Kapaleeshwarar temple, they invite me and give me temple honours. We should respect each other's place of worship.'

When the Prince visited Ayodhya, after the Babri Masjid incident, he met many people who told him, 'We were happily living together and it is because of the politicians that Ayodhya has been ruined. We are together in happiness and sorrow, they are trying to divide us in the name of religion.'

Noticing our fast emptying plates, the Prince urged us to replenish them. 'More ... have some more!'

My son was only too happy to comply but the sandwiches proved tricky. He was on his best behaviour; how did one pick up a sandwich with a spoon?

The Prince was delightfully informal. 'Use your fingers, son!' he said kindly. 'When God has given us fingers, why use a spoon?'

One might say that of all the twelve Nawabs of Arcot, and the eight Princes, Nawab Wallajah was the most important in terms of shaping both the future of the Carnatic and that of the British in India. After he died in 1795, his debts that amounted to millions of pagodas (the currency in use then) and pounds were ultimately settled in 1801 by the British taking over the entire Carnatic in exchange for his dues.

In 1855, the British went a step further and took away Chepauk palace as well employing the charade of a fairly held auction. A few years later when the twelfth Nawab died without an heir, Dalhousie's preposterous policy of annexation under the Doctrine of Lapse came into effect. No heir in the direct line of succession; end of the dynasty; territories annexed by the East India Company. It meant that most of the southern peninsula would no longer be in the hands of the Arcot family. When the late twelfth Nawab's regent and uncle Azim Jah protested and hired legal representation, he did get a title for his pains. In 1867, Queen Victoria named Azim Jah *Amir e Arcot* or the Prince of Arcot. And though there were several honours the Prince was entitled to, including passing on the title to his heir, apart from a specified monthly payment, effectively the family had lost all hold on the territories, civil and military administration of the *entire* Carnatic.

'*Sab chheen liya.* They looted us. They took our help and left us with nothing,' said the current Prince, the eighth.

The grand and majestic Chepauk palace was put to mundane use by the British, as government offices, which continues to this day. Hidden from the public eye behind newer, uglier structures, subject to neglect and a lack of maintenance, the palace that cost the Nawab his entire kingdom was badly damaged – Khalas Mahal by fire in 2012, and a portion of the roof of Humayun Mahal collapsed in 2013.

Meanwhile, in 1876, Amir Mahal, 'the British built it on our own land', was occupied by the second Prince Sir Zahir-ud-daula Bahadur and since then has been the residence of the Prince of Arcot.

'Come, I'll show you around the Durbar Hall.' My son and I eagerly followed him out of his office.

While we climbed the stairs to reach the first floor, his staff raced ahead to switch on the wall lights, lamps and single glass-globe chandeliers. And soon we were in a fully carpeted, well-lit hall that served as a reception area for those occasions when the Prince entertained formally, and red-and-gold seating on a slightly raised dais at the far end allowed him to grant audience in the old-fashioned way. Further inward was the banquet room, the walls covered with photographs of the many famous people who had visited Amir Mahal; the President of India, the Archbishop of Canterbury, the Crown Prince of Saudi Arabia, the head of the Kanchi Kamakoti Peetham. 'It is the first time the head of the Kanchi Mutt, Sri Jayendra Saraswati was visiting a Muslim home. He acknowledged the many gifts of land made by Nawab Wallajah in Kanchipuram.'

Large, almost life-size, paintings of his ancestors in large gilt-edged frames hung on the walls, all wearing the Arcot *sarpech* or turban-jewel, their swords prominent. 'This is Nawab Wallajah with Major General Stringer Lawrence. This is the second Prince, and this the fifth Prince...'

It was interesting that while the men in all the formal portraits wore ceremonial clothes, the photos of the Prince showed him in contemporary attire – *bandhgala*, suits, or kurta-pyjama-waistcoat, sans bejeweled armbands or necklaces. In a photograph taken with Nehru, he was a little boy in shorts.

'At what age did it dawn on you that you were heir to all this history, and the next Prince of Arcot?'

His answer was refreshing in its frankness. 'What does it mean – Prince of Arcot? It is an honourable position. It is not a Prince by state or throne or ornaments. *That* the British took from us.' He glanced upwards and said, '*He* has given it to me. No Raja, no Nawab is dropped from the sky, this is all made in the world, of the world. It is His grace, when so many princely families had their title abolished, that this one continues.'

He then explained, 'This title the British gave … "Prince!" had several honours that go with it, and those privileges and courtesies still continue. There are some tax exemptions. I am not a politician, but in terms of the state protocol I have a high ranking and a diplomatic passport. My father, the late Prince, was buried with full state honours when he passed away in 1993.'

The first Prince Azim Jah was also made a 'political pensioner' and a stipend given to him and descendents of the Nawabs of Arcot in perpetuity, collectively known as the 'Carnatic Stipend'. The Collector of Madras acts as paymaster and a liaison between the Prince and the Government. In one of those coincidences that are not rare in India, my father was once Collector of Madras, in the sixties, and interacted with Mohammad Abdul Ali's father, the then Prince.

The place of First Nobleman of the Muslim community in south India is granted to the Prince of Arcot. In this capacity, the current Prince works actively through his religious endowments, giving scholarships, feeding people, and helping poor families.

In 1990, he was one of the founding members of Harmony India, which had a thirty-two member committee drawn from all religions. The aim was to build communal harmony and through inter-faith dialogue develop a deeper understanding of different belief systems.

'All religions say the same thing. We all have to die one day and answer God. This life is only a transit. Muslim or Hindu, there should not be that feeling of difference. If you are a Hindu, what difference does it make? We are made by the same God, one Creator. You and I are happily sitting and eating here … There should be harmony and peace. We are lucky we live in Tamil Nadu. People are not bothered about communalism. In that way Tamil Nadu, and within it, Madras is the best in India.'

Soon it was time to leave. The Prince's old-world manners, that he finds increasingly vanishing in the city, led him to escort us all the way to the entrance, solicitously enquiring if I had transport home. His car, parked in the spacious portico of a height to admit elephants, had a revolving red light fixed on it; of all his perks, I thought to myself, I would like that the most.

There was a lot to think about as my son and I drove away. What had begun as a factory for the sourcing of cheap cotton, a place of trade, had arrogated to itself the right to meddle in the affairs of Indian princes and ultimately rule the Indian subcontinent, subjugating its people. The ideas and events that triggered such an imperial expansion happened in the few kilometres between Fort St. George and Chepauk Palace. Even Robert Clive, long acknowledged as the early founder of the Company's rise to power, was at first a mere writer, or factor, at Fort St. George. Ironically, Chepauk would be known to the modern world for its association with cricket and not so much the Nawab whose palace grounds it once was.

5

Of Old and New Traditions

'"Aiyyayo, if I had known, I would not have given Out!"'
V Ramnarayan

Growing up in Madras, it was in observing the absolute passion reserved for cricket in this city that I understood my family was unusual – from Mars perhaps. At school, on match days, an intrepid classmate would sneak a pocket transistor into class and scores were passed in a series of Chinese whispers. Cards with stamp sized photographs and outdated statistics were gazed at longingly, especially those with Imran Khan on them. Slips, mid-on, gully belonged to an esoteric language I understood only dimly.

The cousins, uncles, aunts, grandparents, distant relatives, visiting neighbours whom I encountered at my friends' homes … they all contributed to the great excitement that preceded a match, especially in the pre-Doordarshan days. In my home, there were just the three of us – mother, father, child. Not enough of a quorum for endless discussions about the game, nor jubilant trips to the stadium with food for an army packed in the dicky of the car, and most certainly not an actual attempt at playing.

Years later, I accessed the cricket experience as a parent, encountering a particular middle-class mindset that went with it.

My son Chinmaya, who had only just grown out of toddler-hood by the year 2000, suddenly started winning gold medals in track events. The 100 metre dash was particularly suited to his high energy levels and soon I had a handful of medals with colourful ribbons and a bunch of certificates.

It meant long sessions at Sportus, a local sports-gear shop, buying track shoes that fit; packing snacks and beverages to last the day; accompanying him to long, dusty practice sessions; carrying his kit; cheering madly when he ran and consoling him when he fell and scraped a knee. All of a sudden, I was the mother of a sportsman. Seven years old, 3 feet 9 inches tall, but a sportsman nonetheless.

Over the next two years, as he grew taller, he lost his advantage of speed in running. He then developed an interest in cricket.

Back to Sportus. We bought a lovely bat. Pads and gloves and whites and spiked shoes. And a long, narrow kit-bag to carry them in. He wore all of these at the first session with the coach. He looked very grown-up but he was recognizably the same boy. And then he put on his carbon helmet with the face guard, and before my eyes, my son turned into Sachin Tendulkar.

I began to dream of a life spent in locker rooms and stadiums. Mother of Chinmaya the cricketer; that's how I would be known. I would travel around the world, escorting him from one match to another. Nothing, not even the coach's embarrassment as he told me to equip my son with an 'abdominal' protector, could shake that dream.

The coach thought Chinmaya had potential, the makings of a pace bowler. So we graduated to a cricket academy, attending camp there at the peak of summer. To beat the heat, camp started at dawn. I found myself sleep-driving my son to this far-off place, returning to pick him up by 10 a.m., when the sun was already high in the sky and blazing. The boy got roasted in the sun, his skin turning dark brown and the whites of his eyes standing out like two saucers.

And now we were ready to play matches in a sort of informal league, children drawn from other camps to form teams. Even further away from home, in the scorching heat of May, we assembled at a vast field in Nandanam that I did not know existed. White shirts and white elasticized pants, green grass, thirst, the heat and the dust. The boys, aged between ten to twelve, played; their parents and relatives competed.

Every other player was assessed, judged, evaluated for the threat they offered their offspring. It was an education in a peculiar kind of middle-class anxiety and competitiveness. The same kind that led parents to spend scarce resources on coaching classes for the IIT and other entrance exams, condemning their kids to long hours of study without respite, burying them under the weight of their expectations.

What was also clear, from their informed conversations, was that just like everything else in the country, talent alone did not automatically guarantee a place in any cricket team – local, state or national. There were strings always waiting to be pulled.

Here, in this setting, my dream seemed insubstantial, silly even, compared to the fierce ambitions on display. It was all too *real*, the raw need, the craving for the great leap in material circumstances that a gifted child could achieve for them. *That* was not my dream.

During the last match of the summer, my son chased a ball to the periphery of the grounds. On the scanty grass there, he saw a skull, with some flesh stuck to the yellowing bone.

Something changed in him; his interest switched permanently to football.

He was a teenager now, fast approaching six feet in height. He had grown out of his track-pants and sneakers. Shin guards, long socks, cleats, an arsenal of footballs – Sportus owed much of its profits to me. It moved to a more spacious store.

My son was now a sharp-eyed goalie; and I, the retired mother of a sportsman.

If the love for cricket is an integral part of the city, then V Ramnarayan's experience shows just how well this love was integrated within the family, with the stream of life. Accustomed to carrying forward traditions, particularly that of Carnatic music, it was easy to fashion a new cricket tradition, absorbing its lore into that of the city.

In his own life, Ramnarayan was to bring together the two great loves of the city – cricket and Carnatic music – into his writing.

Tall, well-built, Ramnarayan is in his sixties now, and we met at the 164-year-old Madras Cricket Club, the crown holding the Kohinoor that is the Chepauk stadium. Walking past founder Arbuthnot's portrait, we settled down in the silent pavilion. Sipping on MCC's signature drink 'Cricket', part 7 Up, part Fanta, my eyes flitted over the empty tiers that on a match-day are surcharged with energy, anticipation and the high-decibel buzz of fifty thousand people.

It was here that Buchi Babu Naidu, who had grown up watching cricket matches at Chepauk, and practising the game in his home Lakshmi Vilas set in 20 acres in Luz, confronted the whites-only policy of the MCC. Even when it condescended to play with 'native' teams, they were not allowed entry to the pavilion and had to change their clothes or lunch al fresco, under the trees.

With the self-confidence born of his immense family wealth, social position, westernized lifestyle and an education imparted by British governesses, he decided to form his own club, the Madras United Cricket Club (later called the Madras United Club or MUC) *with* a pavilion open to all, in 1888. That determination led to his creating a team, even if it meant providing most of its dhoti-clad members with cricket gear brought from abroad. Came the triumphant moment when MUC was invited to play against the MCC and at Buchi Babu's insistence, the team had lunch inside the pavilion. It would take many more decades and the imminent certainty of Independence before the MCC finally opened its doors to Indians.

That Irwin-designed pavilion no longer exists.

The Chepauk stadium was officially named the MA Chidambaram stadium, though people still refer to it as 'Chepauk'.

The recently renovated stands with folding seats, fabric tensile roofs and gaps welcoming the sea breeze were a clear improvement on the earlier heavy-pillared concrete oven. A few kilometres away from Fort St. George where it all began, Chepauk upholds the city's pre-eminence on the map of Indian international cricket.

Gazing across the green field at work being done on the pitch, Ramnarayan reminisced about the time before the stadium existed at all.

'The pitch has a bit of bounce on it. It is a lively, sporting wicket, good for both bowlers and batsmen. Maybe because of the soil, being close to the sea. When it was tree-lined, it had a completely different surface … It was a beautiful cricket space before the stands came up.'

The crowd that came to watch was knowledgeable about the game. Marina, the home ground of Presidency College nearby, perhaps attracted larger crowds because it was so close to the road. Milling around the boundary line, perched on walls, seated on scooters, they commented non-stop on the action. In a city where there was always 'time to stand and stare', passers-by would stop to watch local matches in those days before television brought international cricket to your drawing room. Some spent the whole day travelling from match to match, broadcasting the scores of the ones they had just come away from.

The man in the crowd was not just a spectator. He had probably grown up playing cricket, as had Ramnarayan.

'I come from a family of cricketers. Some of them studied law whether they practised at the court or not, some were interested in Carnatic music and many of them played cricket. My grand-uncle, PS Ramachandran, a pace bowler, was in the inaugural Ranji trophy match between Madras and Mysore, back in 1934. My father and my uncle lived together in a two-storeyed house on Murrays Gate Road. Between that house and two others on Eldams Road, where PSR and his brother lived, there was no compound wall, so my siblings, cousins and I enjoyed a large play area.'

A huge open land in the neighbourhood, which is now Venus Colony, was usurped by the cricket-warriors. 'My family ran a cricket club called Mylapore Recreation Club, so there was always a kit available for us, and old balls. We never paid for anything.' Unlike most other children, Ramnarayan and his cousins did not have to graduate from tennis balls to 'real' cricket.

Ramanarayan grew up in the fifties surrounded by talk about cricket. 'My uncle was *The Hindu's* cricket correspondent, and there was always cricket talk around. He once nearly killed an impertinent cousin who made disparaging remarks against England, the team Uncle supported. There was a strict code among the cousins, the older ones tending to dominate you. You had to be of stern stuff, and I somehow managed to survive.'

It took time for him to understand where his talent lay.

'Like most of our generation, I tried everything as a kid but I was a bowler at heart. No one paid much attention to my bowling. Because my father worked all over India, and our family went with him, my brothers and I never settled down to play inter-school cricket.'

During his last year in school, Vidya Mandir, playing cricket in the sun, during all of the forty minutes for lunch break, Ramnarayan discovered that he had a talent for off spin. 'I was unplayable on the uneven surface – a dangerous place for a batsman.'

It turned out to be no fluke when Ramnarayan tried the same grip and action with senior cricketers during summer net practice. The batsmen found it difficult to play him. 'I joined Vivekananda College for my pre-University course but was not selected for the team. Ram Ramesh the captain was feeling bad, and he introduced me to Jai Hind CC in the local league for which I played.' Ramesh also put in a word with the selectors and made sure Ramnarayan was included in the Presidency College team when he moved there to do his degree course.

Encouraged by Jai Hind captain, S Raman, 'I did so well, I was picked for the MCA Colts team and went to Bombay. It was a wonderful experience to play some of the best cricketers in India there. In the opener at Brabourne stadium, the great Vinoo Mankad, just retired from Test cricket led Cricket Club of India against us and handed us our caps. He looked very distinguished. It was like royalty talking to us.'

In the game, Ramnarayan came on early, when the ball was still new, and straightaway caused problems for the batsmen, one of whom, Arvind Apte, was a Test opener. Just then his captain insisted that he toss the ball higher, and promptly took Ramnarayan off when he was hit for a boundary or two. 'Young bowlers of Madras always had to contend with advice offered gratis by anyone a day older, and I normally knew how to sift the grain from the chaff, but not this time. I did not get another bowl till the last match of the tour, and I did not get any opportunities for the next five years despite consistent performances in college and league cricket. The way I was bowling those days, a good showing on that tour could have given me a fairy tale launch.'

Back in Madras, studying Chemistry in Presidency College, he found other mentors such as VV Rajamani. 'My bowling came of age there. I grew in confidence as an off spinner. My spin twin CS Dayakar and I were perhaps the most successful pair in intercollegiate cricket, but were never picked for the university, my entry blocked by the world class Venkataraghavan, already a Test bowler. Neither of us could even get into one of the City Colleges team. It gave us perverse pride to make waves in college matches without being rewarded.'

On matting wickets, Ramnarayan obtained sharp turn and steep bounce. Occasionally, some Tamil Nadu batsmen enlisted his services as a net bowler in preparation for matches in the matting wickets of Andhra and Kerala. 'I bowled my heart out, and derived much innocent pleasure from rattling the batsmen's composure, instead of giving them confidence!'

In his final year, Ramanarayan could have played for Madras University as Venkataraghavan had by then graduated, but 'I was doing badly academically and in consultation with my parents decided to abstain from cricket to prepare for the university exams'.

Spending a year as an apprentice sub-editor in *The Indian Express*, Ramnarayan went back to college to do an MA in political science. It was only in the final year of his MA course, when he captained the college team, that he eventually played for the University, after two consecutive years of success for City Colleges versus District Colleges.

'So this is where my career stood when I left Chennai. It was another uphill struggle in Hyderabad and I was twenty-eight before I made my Ranji Trophy debut. I never played for my own state, Tamil Nadu.'

With the wisdom that comes with years, Ramnarayan described the appeal of cricket, and the way it was played in his generation.

'The intellectual aspects of the game attracted us. It is played in so many forms, has so many kinds of bowling, speed, swing, seam, spin, so many specialist positions in batting or fielding, different kinds of playing surfaces, weather conditions. All these make cricket so fascinating, and varying conditions can tilt the balance in favour of one team or the other. I think the mental aspect of the game may be more attractive to the southerner, while up north, they are much more natural, aggressive players.'

On the grounds, facilities were markedly primitive. 'The shade of a large tree served as the dressing room. The gloves, leg guards and shoes worn by most of us often performed a psychological rather than protective role given that we could not afford high quality gear. In fact, you needed contacts abroad or access to visiting Test cricketers to buy bats and other gear from them at fancy prices. A Gunn and Moore, Gray-Nicolls or Autograph bat could cost upwards of a hundred rupees and that was a lot of money for the average cricketer.'

Lunch was not fancy at all. 'It involved a hurried dash to Ratna Café, Udipi Sukha Nivas, Shanti Vihar, Udipi Home or Dasaprakash and back, depending on the venue of the match. When I see the fancy drinks cart of today, I remember the countless glasses of unboiled, unfiltered and often multi-hued water we drank. It was stored in mud pots or brought in buckets that resembled relics!'

The spirit on the field was one where a bowler could openly appreciate a batsman's stroke even if he had just been hit for a six. Humour was constant, so also camaraderie. 'My father's cousin, a fast bowler for the state, would appeal for an out, get the decision and then chastise the umpire, "*Idhukku poyi* out *kuduthiyai* ... You gave an out for this? It wasn't an out."' The cricket-map of the city was dominated by Mylapore, Triplicane and Egmore onwards, grudgingly accommodating Adyar and Mambalam later on. The Marina, Loyola, Somasundaram grounds were as well populated as Chepauk. A true fan knew the short-hand ... *danda* out=bad decision, *azhukku* batsman= ugly-strokes batsman, *poi* bowling=bowling more for show than spin, *manga*=chucking balls as though aiming a stone at a mango, and the hilarious grease for crease.

Regarding his generation, and even his seniors, 'We were not extremely athletic. Fielding was at best an unavoidable nuisance and the slips were the preserve of seniors, with the babies of the team banished to the distant outposts of long leg and third man. Fast bowling was too close to real work, left best in the hands of those endowed with more brawn than brain! Though brilliant strokemakers and spin bowlers in local cricket, we were considered no-hopers when it came to locking horns with the more robust if less stylish combatants from Delhi or Bombay.'

For an average Tamil 'curd-rice cricketer', two things mattered a lot – the aesthetics of his playing and his intelligence. 'We never appreciated workman-like batsmen. We preferred an orthodox leg spinner such as VV Kumar, whose art was visible over someone like Anil Kumble, a match winner but not a crowd pleaser. Kapil Dev was a great favourite, with his stylish aggression. In the same vein, stylish batsman Gundappa Viswanath was preferred to the great Sunil Gavaskar, and his unbeaten 97 against the West Indies in 1975 is still rated as one of the greatest innings at Chepauk by those who watched it.'

The nuances described by Ramnarayan have to be seen against the larger context of sheer enjoyment of the game. Of course Gavaskar was a favourite, as demonstrated by the frenzied nine thousand strong crowd that turned up to watch him play during the Buchi Babu Tournament in 1971. And this was not even Chepauk; in a first for the great batsman, he had to be escorted by the police to the wicket at the Loyola College grounds!

Ramnarayan described a certain local mentality that can inhibit a budding cricketer. 'Hats off to anyone who has done well in Tamil Nadu cricket. It is very difficult to make it here, and encouragement is measured – for fear of swollen heads, maybe? In any field, I think we have that tendency ... We need approval from elsewhere, like MS Subbulakshmi singing at the UN. But once you win that approval, they will not let you down. That's our other quality.'

The composition of a team has also undergone change. 'Though Brahmins still seem to dominate the game, earlier, there were many non-Brahmins and Anglo-Indians who played, cricket enabled the inter-mingling of castes.' In one of Ramnarayan's articles there is a hilarious description of his grand-uncle whose top-knot would come undone while bowling, and whose orthodox mother insisted on his having a purifying bath after Jardine, great no doubt but still a foreigner, shook his hand. 'Currently, among the kids who play league cricket, it is more a question of class than caste.

'Here, fathers drop their kids by car at the grounds. We do not have much steel in us. That is why we have won the

Ranji Trophy only twice. You need to be a Bombay chap catching two trains to play, lugging your heavy kit along. Or spend years in a sports hostel like some of the cricketers in the North.'

And for that reason, 'We do not find a Dalit kid coming up easily in cricket or any sports. Very difficult for them to even believe in themselves. They have to be tough to survive competition from more privileged children.'

Even so, there were a few notorious teams such as the Appiah Chettiar Memorial and Singara Velar CC in the eighties and nineties, whose many players were fishermen from Triplicane. 'They were good kids with the angst that society is against them. They had to be disciplined but had a lot of raw talent.'

The untiring raconteur that is Ramnarayan launched into some marvellous anecdotes. 'A batsman from one of these teams once got out in a league game. He returned with his head tonsured and batted again under a new name! Then, there was my redoubtable friend – let's call him Raju. Batsmen were nervous when he was fielding close-in because he issued dire warnings to no one in particular. Once in a match at Ramakrishna Mission School, I was the non-striker when Raju was declared LBW, and he walked away staring hard at the umpire. When I informed the umpire who the batsman was, he started trembling, "*Aiyyayo*, if I had known, I would not have given out!"'

We returned to the trajectory of Ramnarayan's career. In December 1970, he joined the State Bank of India as a probationary officer through a competitive process, not as a cricket recruit, though he could still play cricket for the bank's team.

'The cricket season starts in July. I wasted a few months waiting for the job, and to play for SBI.' He was about twenty-three now, and players younger than him had already made the grade years before, reaching the state team.

Ramnarayan was posted to a small town, Anakapalle, in Andhra Pradesh where he missed cricket intensely. The only connection he had with the game was listening to the radio commentary on Sunil Gavaskar's glorious exploits in the West Indies in his debut series. When in January 1971 the Madras University team came to play at Visakhapatnam, twenty miles away, he would catch a bus every weekend to watch them play and return on Monday, emotionally replete.

By a stroke of luck, the captain of the SBI team in Visakhapatnam, Satyadev, hearing about Ramnarayan, invited him to play there. Ramnarayan was thrilled, only to receive, days later, a telegram that said: Match Cancelled.

Transferred to Vijayawada and on the verge of shifting there, Ramnarayan received another cryptic telegram: Report to Personnel Department on the 1st. When he reached the Department in Hyderabad, to his surprise and delight, he was informed by a listless Personnel officer, ' "The cricket fellows want you." He said it with such contempt!' guffawed Ramnarayan. 'It was so exciting to be there on account of my cricket.'

Although posted in Hyderabad, it took him two more years to actually play for SBI. Again the delay, again the frustration. 'I almost gave up.' It was his SBI teammates who kept Ramnarayan's morale high with constant encouragment. 'Amazingly, they always spoke of me as an India prospect even before I was picked for Hyderabad.'

At the age of twenty-eight, late by cricketing standards, Ramnarayan finally played for Hyderabad, and in the Ranji trophy with renowned cricketers such as ML Jaisimha, MAK Pataudi and Abbas Ali Baig.

'Many of us toil hard without expectation of reward. My nature was like that. You could say I was philosophical about it. Though I was always a positive bowler, my disappointments had given me a negative mindset. I never seriously believed I would make it to the Indian team.'

Ramnarayan never played for India, though he was in the official list of Test probables before the 1977-78 Australia tour. The best he played was Duleep and Deodhar Trophy cricket for South Zone and the Irani Cup for Rest of India.

There is a tendency to venerate only those few who make it to the Indian team, but Ramnarayan's story illustrates how luck and politics also play a role and reminds us of the city's vibrant cricket circuit, indeed culture, that exists away from the more publicized, financially lucrative games played by the national team.

Life continues despite our unfulfilled dreams, and when Ramnarayan left SBI and was later unceremoniously dumped by selectors, he was 'embittered for a brief period. Suddenly, it was difficult to watch the game I loved so much.'

What he did not know was that he had a career in journalism ahead of him. He returned to Madras.

'I love the city. The cultural orientation of the city is something we do not realize when young. I still remember the 1960s when Pandit Ravi Shankar played past midnight at the Music Academy, after saying "Happy New Year" to the audience. Can you imagine that in staid old Madras where everyone went to bed at 9 p.m., he had a full audience!'

Ramnarayan is now the Editor of *Sruti*, a magazine devoted to classical music and dance. He talked about the presence of Carnatic music in his life; how, as a child, time not spent playing cricket and a host of other games or reading was spent absorbing classical music.

'It was always around. My mother is a trained vocalist, with a nice voice, and very good teachers. Which Brahmin household did not have a girl learning Carnatic music? One of my male cousins and I learnt alongside our sisters. Unfortunately, I dropped out as the music lessons clashed with cricket.'

At a time when there was no television, nor computers and the distractions of the internet, the joy of summer holidays lay in the gathering of cousins at Ramnarayan's maternal grandparents' house in Trivandrum. 'Every Friday, the elders gathered around the deity and sang for an hour or two. Everyone knew a *krithi* or another. Some were off-key but it did not matter. As a result of this practice, *Mamava Pattabhirama* became the family anthem at weddings, some thirty of us singing together. That atmosphere of reverence to music was there. You did not speak, you listened. It was expected of you.

'My father was a member of RR Sabha. As a bank officer, he invariably worked long hours, which meant that I attended most of the concerts there. It is very difficult for a ten-year-old to sit and listen to a *kutcheri* concert for three hours, but it never occurred to me to get up and leave midway. I heard all the greats of Carnatic music ... Ariyakudi, Semmangudi, Maharajapuram, Madurai Mani Iyer, MS, MLV ... I would go alone, buy a bus ticket, get down at the Mylapore tank and walk to RR Sabha. In the late fifties, no one worried about you.'

And so, by osmosis, hearing these greats, or an aunt hum in the kitchen, or an uncle sing in front of the puja for an hour, Ramnarayan acquired '*kelvi gnaanam*' or an intricate understanding of the music obtained only by sustained listening over time.

This was to help when he married Gowri, grand-daughter of the noted freedom fighter and writer Kalki Krishnamurty, and became part of the inner family circle of the great singer MS Subbulakshmi.

'Months before our wedding, my future mother-in-law and Gowri and I attended MS's concert at the University Centenary auditorium. I must have impressed with my identification of ragas by fluke, particularly when I picked Nadanamakriya over Sensuruti towards the end of the concert. Phew!'

MS Subbulakshmi bore the initial M for Madurai, where she was born, but it may as well have been Madras for she lent lustre to the city by her very presence. Artistes of her calibre are born but infrequently and it was Ramnarayan's privilege to hear her sing in many informal settings and to spend time with her.

'It was a great experience to have known her as a person. So humble, but she knew what she was doing when she sang, it was not just a gift.'

Known for contributing her concert earnings to various charitable causes, Subbulakshmi's simplicity extended to her personal life as well. 'She had just eight silk saris to wear at her concerts and eight for home wear. When a ninth sari got added, she promptly gave away one of the older ones.' This was an iconic lady whose choice of sari colour led to it being named 'MS blue', and countless women rushing to own one.

'We knew the MS repertoire rather well.' An under-statement, for wife Gowri actually sang in concerts with MS, providing support. Of those gems, some of his favourites were Shyama Sastri's Bhairavi *swarajati* and *Durusuga* in Saveri, Dikshitar's *Meenakshi Memudam* in Gamakakriya and some 'wonderful Annamacharya krithis tuned by Kadayanallur Venkataraman'.

Thus immersed in the best possible musical tradition, it is not surprising that in 1983 Gowri and Ramnarayan persuaded his uncle Pattabhiraman to start a magazine Sruti devoted to Carnatic music and dance.

'He saw it as an international magazine, not limited to just Carnatic music in Madras. We carried interviews with DK Pattamal, U Srinivas, Lakshmi Viswanathan and Sonal Mansingh in the inaugural issue. It helped that Gowri had a wide network among musicians and many of them were friends.'

Sruti played an important role in documenting the biographies and perspectives on art of the best of musicians, thereby recording many oral histories that would have otherwise been lost to time. For anyone writing about music or dance, the Sruti archives are a must, for a great many nuggets of information are to be found in its pages.

'My uncle loved talking endlessly about the merits and demerits of various singers. He had a salon at home and people came to sit and chat. He had a sense of mission with Sruti but he was gossipy too. Many of the readers liked that, though I did not. It mirrored the talk outside.'

Pattabhiraman passed away in 2002 and five years later, Ramnarayan took over, rather reluctantly, as the Editor of Sruti. 'I was not at all sure I was the right person to do it. While I hugely respect many artists, I don't enjoy being in the middle of what is essentially an incestuous world, I try to stay apart from it.'

Soon Ramnarayan realized anew what a tremendous contribution Sruti had made to the arts in the first two decades of its existence. To record and narrate the lives of the greatest of musicians and dancers, the writers themselves had to know a lot about the subject. 'It is difficult now to find the kind of experts Pattabhi was able to collect around him, developing a superb resource base to tap into. Most of them have passed away.'

However, 'when you read all the old issues, you still find scope for improvement, and we do try to benefit from the expertise and sage advice of our living greats.'

What pleases him is the esteem in which Sruti is held. It takes seriously the idea of raising issues central to the arts. One area is, of course, the famed 'Season' that traditionally spanned the Tamil month of Margazhi but now bulges out at both ends to encompass December and January. Ostensibly about celebrating the arts, it's also the time to catch up with friends, flaunt the best of one's Kanjeevaram saris and wander from *Sabha* to Sabha tasting the caterer's delicacies.

'The quality is erratic. On a good day you get some excellent music. Three concerts a day at the Music Academy – could be programmed in a different way, maybe a pre-season show. As for lecture demonstrations, maybe the Sabhas should collectively hold them in one place with longer sessions. The spirit should be that this is the most important festival we have, therefore let us all get together and plan it in a better way.'

The thick moustache of his younger days replaced by a grey beard and longer hair, the dashing cricketer in Ramnarayan yielded to the knowledgeable *rasika*, presiding over felicitations and award ceremonies. 'I love cricket but music seems to have taken over my life!' And yet the two worlds are so apart, that some of his cricketer buddies have no idea of this other aspect to him.

The afternoon sun fell like fire on the lower part of the tiers, proof that anyone braving that had to really enjoy the game. A group of sportswomen in black tracksuits began to limber up on one side of the turf.

In a recently played IPL, Ramnarayan had been plied with cocktail idlis and other bizarre delicacies in the hospitality box, dazed by the incongruity of cheergirls at Chepauk, while the home team Chennai Super Kings won a thrilling last ball finish against Royal Challengers Bangalore. The ground itself, with its megawatt lighting and silken green surface, seemed to have banished temporarily the heat, dust and mugginess of a normal day in Madras. The moneyed crowds were a far cry from the spectators of old who thronged below the hardy trees, lunch packed in their tiffin *dabbas*.

'It will be nice if T20 plays a limited role. Many of us don't like the culture it has spawned. Air-conditioned enclosures, 7-star culture, rubbing shoulders with celebrities … it is unreal. Test cricket is more democratic. The filmstar has to sit with you and watch. Here it is a symbol of upward mobility for you, where you are actually cut off from cricket.'

It does help cricketers to make a mark, but it is seen as an easy passport to success. 'A youngster can go straight into T20, make big money, and not even aspire to play Test cricket. There are some players who vanish after the T20 season. T20 is good fun though, it even helps identify talent from unexpected pockets, lets youngsters rub shoulders with the game's greats. The boundaries are smaller and the bats are getting better, so the bowler has to be very inventive.'

That said, 'The game will die out if we neglect Test cricket, with its superior technical skills, twists and turns and second-innings comebacks. At the same time, it is a challenge to keep five-day cricket alive in the face of dwindling spectator interest.'

As we left the unoccupied stadium, Ramnarayan saluted the spirit of Chepauk crowds. 'They are knowledgeable and interested in the lore and the personalities of the game. They want the better side to win.'

If in 1997 the crowd got to its feet and clapped for Saeed Anwar's outstanding 194, in 1999 it went one better and gave a standing ovation to the Pakistani Test team that snatched victory from the jaws of defeat. Touched, the Pakistanis ran a lap of honour and later Javed Miandad acknowledged it in words: 'Salaam Chennai'.

6

Enriching Cultures

*'San Thome is one of the oldest bastions of Catholicism,
with over two thousand years of Christianity.'*
Dr Beatrix D'Souza

While we had moved to Shastri Nagar, our connection with San Thome had not ended. I studied there at Rosary Matriculation, a school for girls run by the Franciscan Missionaries of Mary. San Thome was packed with churches and Catholic-run schools.

I was taken to school with the other members of our carpool, some of us completing the last stages of wearing shoes or tying ribbons in the car.

It was a long, winding road that led past an open air settlement of gypsies or *narikuravas*, over the Adyar river, and into San Thome. To our right, the river met the sea, its estuary flanked on either side by dense foliage where birds flocked to rest at sunset. The new Thiru Vi Ka bridge, with two cement lions that seemed to have morphed out of the Ashoka pillar staring down at us, seemed wide compared to the narrow Elphinstone Bridge of wrought-iron that we were used to.

The Portuguese had long settled in San Thome, but by 1662, it was in the possession of the Sultan of Golconda. Except for two years when it was occupied by the French, it remained with the Sultan, then passed to Aurangzeb and the Carnatic.

San Thome would only come under the control of the British in 1749, but not before they fought the French. In 1746, the French won, occupied the Fort, razed part of Black Town and looted what they could. Admiral Labourdonnais promised to give it to the seventh Nawab of Arcot, Anwaruddin, if he helped them against the British. When the French refused to quit Fort St. George, the incensed Nawab sent his son Mahfuz Khan with about ten thousand soldiers to fight the French on the banks of the Adyar river on the outer boundary of San Thome.

The French routed his army with a few hundred trained soldiers equipped with more effective firearms. Dupleix refused to honour Labourdonnais' commitment. Madras might have had an entirely different history if not for the fact that when France and Britain signed the treaty of Aix-la-Chapelle swapping territories, Madras, chiefly the Fort, was handed back by the French in 1749. Mylapore too came under the control of the British.

I now realize that each morning on our way to school we retraced part of the route taken by the French soldiers when they won against Mahfuz Khan.

Passing the Chettinad Palace, the Quibble Island cemetery that scared us with the possibility of ghosts, holding our breath as we crossed the wetlands turned garbage dump, Foreshore Estate where I still had friends, the ornate gates of the Archbishop's house, and the post office to the left, we reached the San Thome Basilica.

Looking in through the great door set in its Gothic facade, one glimpsed wooden pews and a warm light. At the altar, a lotus bloomed at the feet of Jesus, as he stood with his arms wide open in love. Two peacocks kept him company.

In the early sixteenth century, the Portuguese, excited by finding the tomb of Saint Thomas, built a larger church adjoining it. They also named the area, then known as 'Meliapor', Sao Thome after the Saint. At the time, 'Meliapor' or Mylapore, was on the coast, and the Portuguese pushed its boundary inland, so as to secure for themselves a fortified area for trade. A hundred years into the future, Fort St. George would be built to the north, and the Portuguese working in various capacities, valuable for their knowledge of local customs, would be invited to settle in the environs of the Fort. At the end of the nineteenth century, the impressive Cathedral was built in place of the older church, with the tomb central to its architecture.

But as we passed the Basilica, slowing down because of the traffic, our only concern was whether we were late for school or not. A frisson of excitement as we passed St. Bede's, filled with boys, and then we were in school, rushing for assembly. We – Hindu, Muslim, Christian, Parsi, Sikh, all – stood in rows reciting the Lord's Prayer, fervently followed by the sign of the cross. There was a lot to pray for: that it would be a classmate's birthday and I would be treated to Parry's sweets; that the teachers would not 'catch' me for my less than white shoes, and that the day's tests would go well.

In the classrooms, Jesus surveyed our naughty behaviour; a crucifix hung above the blackboard high up on the wall. Stuck at our desks during moral science, we envied the 'katlick' girls who got to leave the classroom for catechism. The envy deepened when, during Mass, they got to form a separate line and accept the Holy Communion. What did the pale white wafer taste like? It was all very mysterious.

Our school shared a porous boundary wall with another school, St. Raphael's. If we finished lunch early, then during the break some of us would make an expedition to the chapel there. Admiring the chubby baby in Mother Mary's arms, dipping our fingers into the holy water font, we devoutly sprinkled it on ourselves before opening the heavy wooden doors. Here, the small, near-naked, remote figure from the walls of our classroom descended, grew into a superhuman size in front of us and it was possible to view the terrible nails driven into his hands, and the enormous one through his feet. Droplets of blood trickled from the crown of thorns, and yet his face was serene.

We were there for a selfish purpose, usually. If there was an exam or test later in the day, it helped to pray to Him. Used to the images of innumerable gods – Krishna, Muruga, Amman, Ganesha – the child's mind absorbed this one into the pantheon as well. Jesus belonged to this world of pristine nuns in white habits and piano-accompanied hymns; when we returned home he no longer presided over our lives.

Because the Cathedral was so close to our school, within walking distance, we took it entirely for granted. Had we known, we might have taken pride in the fact that it was one of the only three churches in the world built over an apostle's tomb. When the school did take us there, what I registered was the cool dark atmosphere inside, the beauty of the stained glass window where Jesus appeared in a vibrant red robe in front of St. Thomas. I hesitated to step on the gravestones paving the sanctuary; it seemed disrespectful.

There was the other reminder of St. Thomas' stay in the area, miles across to the west at St. Thomas Mount where too the Portuguese had built a church in the sixteenth century. When the time came for us to write our board exams, then we needed the extra blessings that only a visit to the Mount could ensure. The school arranged buses to take us there. Part excursion, part pilgrimage, we set off in great spirits.

While Kerala has the distinction of being the place where St. Thomas first set foot in India, founding seven-and-a-half churches and baptizing the world's oldest Christians in the first century AD, Madras is where his life ended. Tradition has it that he travelled to Madras, living here for eight years until his death in 72 AD. San Thome beach, Mylapore, the cave at Little Mount where he is said to have lived, and then finally St. Thomas Mount, our bus route covered the long distance he is said to have walked every day as he preached the message of his Master.

While some of the teachers and students disembarked at the base of the Mount, wanting to climb the 135 steps that led to the top, the rest of us watched the ground fall away as our bus drove further and further up, 300 feet into the air. We were not used to heights; buildings were rarely taller than three or four storeys. From the flat peak, it was thrilling to see the panorama of an unfamiliar part of the city. No wonder the Portuguese used this place to light the giant fires that would guide ships at sea. When a plane flew low and overhead with a deafening roar, we squealed at the sight of its winged belly so close to our heads; the airport was a mile away below.

The sixteenth century church, painted shell-white, was much smaller in scale than the Cathedral, with a single row of pews at the center. I remember being particularly excited about the possibility that the stone cross at the Church of Our Lady of Expectations might bleed while we were there, something that it was said to do on occasion.

While the cross, to our disappointment, never bled when we visited the church, there were other things to occupy our attention – the inscriptions in Armenian, the painting of the Madonna, and the nuns of the convent there who welcomed their sisters from the same order. Standing at the pulpit, reading from the Bible at the request of a teacher, I could feel how intimate the space at the altar was.

Most of our teachers were Christian of whom a few were Anglo-Indian. Until the nineties, the surest way of identifying an Anglo-Indian woman in Madras was by her appearance – wearing a skirt or cotton frock, her legs bare. That would change, just as the nuns themselves would start wearing plain single-colour saris. Gone the habit, gone the veil and scapular, which must have been hot to wear.

Dr Beatrix D'Souza's life is remarkable in the way it touches two ends of a spectrum. Born in 1935, while India was still under British rule, Beatrix – daughter of a musician in the Governor's Band – was brought up within walking distance of Fort St. George, the vortex of British power in the city, and momentous years later stepped into the Parliament as the representative of her community, the only community defined in the Constitution of India.

'What did it feel like?' I asked Beatrix, vicariously enjoying that moment.

'It was overwhelming. What a tremendous responsibility, speaking for a whole community,' she replied. 'Driving to Parliament, I would always say a prayer of thanks. One cannot take it for granted, being an MLA or a nominated Member of Parliament. I took the responsibility very, very seriously.'

'What did you wear?' I couldn't help asking, girl to girl.

'A sari, of course!'

Remembering the large gap of years between us, and that she had been a professor for much of her life, I stopped short of asking what colour.

We were lunching at the Madras Gymkhana Club, where I sampled for the first time in my life a Chinese 'thali'—a tray with assorted servings of noodles, rice and vegetables. If the club had embraced change such as this in its menu, in other areas it retained a colonial world view; the dress code for men did not extend to traditional Indian attire.

Seated at one end of the spacious ballroom, bright sunlight filtering in through the tall doors, Beatrix remembered her childhood.

'My father, Thomas Xavier was in the Governor's Band, they were all Anglo-Indians. Chosen from schools like St. Patrick's, St. Bede's ... Anglo-Indian schools where many of the boys had job-oriented courses, shorthand or music. Music was a part of Anglo-Indian life. Each of the Governor's bandsmen had to know two instruments, one for classical and one for dance music. My father played the saxophone and the bassoon.'

In the early years of the Fort's existence, the Chief Agent of the East India Company, later called the Governor, lived within the Fort, and presided over a common table. Over the years, his residence within the Fort changed several times, and he was given the privilege of living outside the Fort as well. In 1853, Government House was purchased as the residence of Governor Saunders. A cool white building with colonnaded verandahs, Burma-wood rafters, teak doors twelve feet high and marble floors, it was adjacent to Banqueting Hall where the Governor entertained and presided over formal ceremonies and balls.

Beatrix grew up in the vicinity of both. 'We lived in quarters that were part of the Governor's estate. As children we would run about, play there, go up to the Government House or all the way out to the beach. My father named me after Governor, Lord Stanley's daughter.'

Where the Governor went, so did his official entourage, and his Band. And their families. So Beatrix spent six of the hottest months in Ooty. 'In summer, all of us packed up and went by train there. When we arrived at our quarters there, there would be a hot stew of 'English vegetables' waiting for us.'

The weather in Ooty was wonderful and Beatrix and her young friends had much to occupy themselves with. 'There was a log cabin built for one of the Governor's daughters. We would wear sola topees ... keep ourselves warm and trek to the cabin. When it was time to return for lunch, we walked past potato fields, and filled our pockets with small hill guavas. After lunch … we would go down into the valley-like *Khudd* where the servant's quarters were located, to buy roasted peanuts. It was a fantastic childhood.'

The highlight of their stay there was the Ooty flower show. 'We ran there in the morning, when they were arranging the flowers. Later, the band would be playing at one end.'

In 1947, while the community celebrated Independence along with the rest of the country, it was not without a sense of anxiety about their future. 'There was a time just after Independence, whoever had a British father or grand-father, a British passport, left India. For the rest of us, this is our home – why would we want to leave?' Beatrix's family stayed on.

In Madras, capital of the newly created state of Tamil Nadu, carved out of the much larger Madras Presidency, the post of the Governor remained with the official residence now at Raj Bhavan in Guindy, but the Band was dissolved. Along with other musicians playing western instruments, some members were absorbed into the film industry in Madras, as part of the huge orchestra for musical scores, where they quickly learnt Tamil notation and *sa re ga ma* notes. Some played at restaurants. One of Beatrix's uncles, Harry Xavier, was a conductor of the well-known Madras Orchestra Association.

Though the piano was part of the furniture in most Anglo-Indian homes, as also the banjo and the guitar, Beatrix herself did not learn any instrument though her two brothers are professional musicians.

'My uncles found work *here*, playing at the Gymkhana.' Beatrix turned in her seat to point to a recess at the other end of the ballroom. 'That portion there was for the band and, of course, the wooden floor for dancing.'

Since they preferred food sent from home to the sandwiches served at the Gymkhana, Beatrix, by now a teenager, would sometimes accompany her male cousins, bringing her uncles their dinner.

'Though not in the Government House estate, we still lived close by, near the Chepauk stadium, and walked from there to the back boundary of the club, near the tennis courts,' Beatrix gestured to the north-eastern part of the grounds. 'While my uncles played, I would watch all the "white" people dancing, thinking to myself, *Look at these people* ... I was intensely aware of the social exclusion for the Gymkhana only admitted Europeans, though not resenting their presence.'

Today, Beatrix is a member of the club. 'Whenever I come here, I think of my father and uncle. They would have never thought this possible.' And a dream that wasn't hers at the time came true as well. Beatrix became a Member of the Legislative Assembly of Tamil Nadu. 'I attended a party at Raj Bhavan, where the band used to play! Again they could never have imagined that one day, I would be invited a guest of the Governor!'

In 2008, Government House which was linked to the city's history for over two hundred years, both as the garden house owned by the de Madeiros 'Madra' family from which Madras may have derived its name, and as the residence of successive Governors, was demolished. Other buildings in the estate were also brought down, among them Beatrix's childhood home.

'Those quarters have now been demolished to make way for the monstrosity that is the new Assembly building. I wanted to get one or two bricks for remembrance.' In 2011, when the AIADMK government took charge, both the Assembly and the Secretariat returned to their old habitat at the Fort. The new Rs 1,200 crore building meant for the Assembly is being turned into a hospital.

Beatrix herself was familiar with the old Assembly building, having attended sessions there. And in her person, she represented years of history that enabled her to become an MLA.

'There are two things about my community that not all Anglo-Indians know. First, it did not start with the British, but with the coming of Vasco da Gama 500 years ago. So, we as a community grew at the same time the Mughals came into India but unlike the Muslims who are accepted as a very Indian community we were always judged for being the result of inter-racial marriages.'

If the Portuguese followed a policy of encouraging its men to marry local girls, 'the mothers of the community' as Beatrix put it, resulting in the Luso-Indian community that populated Luz and San Thome well before Madras was born, the East India Company actually offered money as an incentive, offering one pagoda on the day of the baby's christening to any local woman who had a child with a man of English descent.

A list of some of the Anglo-Indian surnames reveals French, Dutch, Portuguese, English, Irish, Scottish, Italian and Spanish lines of descent. In Beatrix's own family, there are strains of Irish blood. Her great-grandfather was an Irishman named Garrett, who worked in the railways.

Twirling hakka noodles around her fork, Beatrix continued, 'The second thing is that we had no caste. If the British said "mixed blood", the Indians called us "half-caste". Actually we are a casteless community – the only Christians in India who do not believe in caste, and therefore have no caste problems, no dowry. An Anglo-Indian bride is never overdressed or weighed down in gold. My husband and I never thought it was necessary for our parents to furnish our house … which we did gradually.'

Beatrix was only sixteen when she attended Stella Maris college. 'We are a cent per cent literate community as there were many schools set up only for us, for the children of British officers who died in the war. I was one of the first amongst bands-people to go to college.'

With a degree in Economics and a Masters in Literature, Beatrix started teaching literature at Stella Maris, but was disheartened when her alma mater did not give her a permanent job. 'I went back home in tears. I had thought they would be happy to have me.'

Her father suggested she join Government service, which she did at the young age of twenty-four. She was first posted to Raja's College, Pudukkottai and after being selected by the Madras Public Service Commission, she was posted to Queen Mary's College. 'It was the best thing that happened to me!'

In working, Beatrix was following the example set by other Anglo-Indians, 'the first women to join the work place. The top nurses and matrons in the country were Anglo-Indians. They were a dedicated lot. Most of the executive chiefs of companies, had Anglo-Indians as their top secretaries. Air-hostesses, singers at night clubs, telephone operators. We made good teachers. It was a vocation, teachers were never paid much.'

That sense of vocation helped when it came to Beatrix's job that involved postings outside Madras, and every three years Beatrix had to shift from one town to another. Namakkal, Ponneri, Walajapet … city-bred Beatrix had to face many issues and some prejudice.

To begin with, clothes.

'I wore a dress in Pudukottai … Dresses were so much a part of our culture. We followed all the European fashions – flared skirts, midi, mini – but on the whole Anglo-Indians did not dress vulgarly. If we went to the tailor, no Anglo-Indian girl would say "I want my neck a little bit lower". I myself add lace to a neckline if I find it a bit too low, but my daughter protests, saying "Mamma, who cares?!" Anyway, coming back to Pudukottai, the next morning everyone I met told me exactly where I had been shopping the previous evening and what Missiamma had bought. "*You bought toothpaste, I believe.*"

In small-town Pudukottai, Beatrix stood out because of her dress, her legs displayed where others were covered. So when she moved to even smaller Namakkal, where she was possibly the only Anglo-Indian, she wore saris to work. It was a big change for her, used as she was to the comfort of dresses.

Beatrix does not miss the irony wrought by changing times. What was once the mark of the 'mixed caste', western attire, has now been adopted increasingly by the younger generation in the city. To add to that, in a deliciously incongruous twist, younger actresses and matrons of a certain age have taken to wearing western gowns. 'Film stars wearing slinky dresses in the morning meant for the night! We ourselves are horrified seeing how some of them dress.'

However, in Walajapet she had other problems more pressing than her attire. Lodging, for instance. The rules did not allow the teaching staff to stay in the girl's hostel. Finding a safe, decent place to stay was very difficult, especially for a woman alone. 'When you left the shelter of the college in the evening, you had to roll out your mat and sleep anywhere, until you found a place to rent. Once in temporary lodgings, I had to sleep near an open drain with another colleague.'

Still, her love of teaching kept Beatrix going. 'You couldn't bring your family along, so I would come home to Madras every weekend and go back to Walajapet by the 7 a.m. bus.'

By now, Beatrix was married to Neil D'Souza, to the relief of her grandmother and mother who had admonished her, "Don't marry a caste-boy!" They preferred that we marry our own boys, of our own culture. Anglo-Indians were never keen on their daughters marrying outside the community, European or Indian. When girls had boyfriends they came home, never met clandestinely around the corner. Girls and boys met in a community setting … at church or at dances.'

Again, changing times and increasing westernization meant that what was once seen as scandalous on the part of Anglo-Indians, young unmarried boys and girls being free to intermingle socially sans chaperones, was now part of the reality of the city, from the nineties onwards. But with a difference. For many girls, it was a furtive adventure. 'I have heard of students from other communities who would leave their homes dressed soberly, go to discos, change into miniskirts, smoke, drink and then change clothes again before going back home.'

Beatrix also involved herself with social work within her community, while bringing up her two daughters. In 1991, when she was Head of the Department of English at Presidency College and with two years left to retire, Beatrix embarked on an unusual path. She set her eyes on a seat in the Legislative Assembly.

The Anglo-Indian community is the only one to have a seat in the Legislative Assembly of certain states reserved for its members, and two seats in the Lok Sabha. This was achieved at the time of Independence, thanks largely to the efforts of barrister Frank Anthony, to reassure those who did not emigrate that they were an integral part of the country.

In Beatrix's view, 'Some people stick to preconceived notions that we are a community neither here nor there and pining to go abroad, that we all want to go away to England. Many did leave for Australia, but now Anglo-Indians are getting jobs everywhere and do not want to go out. No Anglo-

Indian feels they should be ashamed of being Anglo-Indian. We are quite happy in our own skin. It is misrepresented in movies. In fact, we were much ahead of our time, pointing the way to a multi-racial, multi-cultural world … in this century, no one thinks of it as mixed blood.'

After years of being involved with the All India Anglo-Indian Association and having worked with Frank Anthony, Beatrix aimed for the position of MLA.

'I told my husband "I like Ms Jayalalithaa, I'm sure she will become Chief Minister. I want to send in my papers for nomination." He was supportive.' Giving up an established career for a new direction in life, would also mean relinquishing a salary of Rs 10,000 to accept the Rs 3,000 allowance given to an MLA. 'My husband said, "Use it for petrol."'

Beatrix described what happened next in her inimitable way. 'She did not ask me to come and see her. I got the call in college. An officer told me I had been nominated. "Madam says you will have to leave your job." The news created a lot of excitement, especially among my students.

'Whenever I met Jayalalithaa I would give her a book. She loved reading. I genuinely like her. I feel she is lonely … It is difficult to be a woman and a politician. Politics is a tough game. If they want to attack you the first thing will be about your character or personal life, not so about a man. I admire her as a woman. She was always accessible to me. I would stand in a whole line of people. As she passed, I would say, "Excuse me, Ma'am" and she would say, "Yes, Dr D'Souza?" The other women MLAs would get jealous!'

Beatrix was an MLA in Tamil Nadu from 1991 to 1996. 'I will always be grateful to her for that.'

The chatter at the neighbouring tables had died down, so also the tinkle of cutlery against china. It was time to leave.

Near the entrance, a polished wooden board named all the Presidents of the club. I loved the fact that at one point rows of British names were followed by Indian ones.

About a month later, I visited Beatrix at her home in San Thome. The area lay barely five kilometres south of the Fort, in the same line, now linked by a smooth tarred road. Thinking of it as a separate enclave, fortified territory, made me understand what distances meant in those days when one travelled by foot or on horseback. Also, it is inconceivable to think of Madras the city without San Thome.

Having left school, there was no reason any more to visit this area, except to drive through it, for four years, on the way to work at Parry's Corner. Nowadays, I took this route infrequently.

The Oceanic hotel was gone, its garden eaten up by concrete. Gone the distinctive whitewashed building that housed Band Box, the laundry store. And lately, gone the grocery store Sealords that had been there forever. The road itself had been widened up to a certain point, which on a winding road known for its narrowness and tendency to get flooded with rain water, was disorienting. Near the spire of the Basilica, appeared a tall brass-coated flagpole ending in a cross, reminiscent in its appearance of the *dhvaja stambha* or flagmast in temples.

Soon I was in a fairly new apartment building, admiring the peacocks carved on Beatrix's Burma-teak front door. 'In honour of Mylapore,' she said. Over sandwiches and whisky-marmalade cake, I heard some wonderful stories from Beatrix.

Having served successfully as an MLA, it was not altogether unimaginable that Beatrix might be nominated a Member of Parliament. 'I went to Delhi to see George Fernandes. He was not there, so I left my bio-data with his PA. Back home, suddenly the phone rang at eleven in the night. "George Fernandes speaking." You know, a call that late in the night … I thought it was a prank. "You are being nominated as MP. I would like you to leave tomorrow by the first flight for Delhi. We'll get your ticket for you." I said, "No Sir, I'll get it myself.""

Beatrix was in a quandary. Her husband had passed away, her children were abroad, she was not very familiar with the process of getting plane tickets, and more crucially, she did not have money at home.

'I did not sleep that night. I borrowed from Mr Daniel, a former colleague at Presidency, who lived nearby. Giving me Rs 10,000, he told me, "I never keep money in the house but I happened to have this amount." Without telling anyone, I set off to Delhi. I was sitting at the airport still wondering if it was a joke.'

The Samata Party was pleased to have Beatrix as its woman MP in 1998. However, Beatrix did feel she owed Jayalalithaa an explanation. 'Let me quote Brutus about Julius Caesar and Rome, *It is not that I loved Jayalalithaa less but that I loved George more.* George was in the Northeast, and he frightened me by saying if I shifted to AIADMK I would lose the nomination. I was in tears. Afterwards, I spoke to her on the phone, saying, "I am really sorry, Ma'am". I owe her a lot.'

Beatrix was a member of the twelfth and thirteenth Lok Sabha.

It resulted in her being unanimously elected President of a union of 3,000 men at the Avadi Ordinance Factory. 'I managed to get the indigenous tanks shifted out for use by the Army, which at that time were using Russian tanks. George Fernandes was Defence Minister and that helped.'

It also gave her a deeply personal moment of triumph: 'One IAS officer had made me cry when he refused to consider my request for a post in Madras after having been transferred all over the State. When I became an MP, he was sitting next to me in the aircraft and I realized I now outranked him.'

From college professor to MP almost overnight, Beatrix had a marvellous time. 'I saw and spoke to famous political leaders whom I had only read about in the newspapers. We were invited to the Prime Minister's residence for breakfast or dinner after a parliamentary session. I had a little car with a red beacon on top. I was thrilled!'

Even better, 'I got to travel all over India on work related to the various Committees I was part of.' The hard work and long hours were compensated by the perks. 'We flew 'J' class, stayed in 5 star hotels, often had an armed escort while sightseeing.' Memorably, 'in Goa we were given *feni* and a packet of cashewnuts! And in Srinagar, we attended three dinners with the same menu and longed for a simple meal.'

One of the few women MPs in Parliament, Beatrix got to see things from an unusual perspective. Whether it was joining all the women in the well of the House at Mamata Banerjee's command, or noticing the fact that Sonia Gandhi spoke little in Parliament, or the jealousies and in-fighting between the women of a party, or that on the day of a vote, the House would be full of unfamiliar faces, Beatrix involved herself keenly in the proceedings. 'I never missed a single day of Parliament.'

A mild, short and plump woman wearing her *pallu* over her right shoulder turned out to be Phoolan Devi. 'She looked like a simple village woman. You would not know she was the bandit, no bandana, pants nor rifle!' Beatrix could not talk to her because she did not know Hindi. 'The lady doctor assigned to the Parliament said Phoolan Devi would cry in her presence, "I hate men. You do not know how much I have suffered, I love children but cannot have them." All she wanted was to lead an ordinary life as a woman.'

When the Empowerment of Women Committee decided to visit the women's jails, Phoolan refused to come. 'She said. "I know what happens. I have been there." When I came back at night, I had difficulty falling asleep, the women's stories ... you take it so personally. Without any trial, in jail for some petty thing...'

Beatrix got some unexpected insights as well. When she stood up to speak about rape, she wanted the definition to be extended to sexual assault 'because when children are assaulted, very often objects are used'. A famous lady MP had admonished her later, 'You should be ashamed of yourself, Betty! Standing up in front of all those men and talking about objects being inserted.' Beatrix was reassured that she had done some good when a young male MP said to her later, 'Ma'am, I never realized this until you spoke, but it is true. The man can get away with assault because of the way rape is currently defined.' Of course, it was to take another decade, and the horrific gang-rape and subsequent death of 'Nirbhaya', before the definition of rape was amended.

Beatrix did try to do as much good as she could. 'I spent money. Usually a Member of Parliament's funds are spent only in the home state. However, the way I saw it, wherever there is an Anglo-Indian, it is our constituency, which was the whole of India. I built some classrooms in Manipur, Tamil Nadu, Kerala and flood-ravaged Orissa.' Across India, she helped old-age homes get ambulances, funded a hostel for child welfare, built roads, and gave money to Anglo-Indian schools to further computer literacy. Granting Rs 10 lakhs to the Department of English, University of Madras for theatre equipment gave her special pleasure as also the grant of Rs 30 lakhs for the Ambedkar Library in Mysore University.

In 2004, her term ended but not her involvement with her community.

'Everyone says that I am one of the best MPs we ever had. I am constantly getting letters from all over asking for help.' Be it jumping into an auto to visit a police station for the first time to recover the body of a boy who had committed suicide, rushing to central jail to release a man before 5 p.m. on Friday so as to avoid his being held over the weekend, helping a woman in distress at the all-women police station, or petitioning for more rape crisis centres, Beatrix will go out of her way to help. 'I am a college professor, I do not know how to deal with some of the more uncooperative policemen.'

Beatrix belonged to one of the oldest churches in the city, St. Lazarus also in San Thome, but has now shifted to the San Thome Cathedral. 'Half of San Thome is owned by the Protestant church and the other half by the Catholic church.'

She talked about the sense of peace immanent in the city. 'San Thome is one of the oldest bastions of Catholicism, with over two thousand years of Christianity. It is because of the Hindus' acceptance that Christianity took root here, because Hindus have no dogma. Especially in the south, there is a tradition and atmosphere of tolerance. Letting each one be. There is no undercurrent of distrust here. In the north, it is something simmering all the time.'

In fact, the Anglo-Indians 'have such a breadth of vision, because we have taken something from both cultures, you absorb something from your Hindu neighbours or your Muslim neighbours. In places like Australia, the Anglo-Indian stands out as a cultured person, your sense of tolerance is already inborn. Anglo-Indians themselves do not realize what they have.'

Through the day, in her home in the heart of San Thome, Beatrix can hear the 'Protestant church bell ringing at a certain time, the Catholic church bells, then the Mohammedan call to prayer.' Outside, in the lanes and byways, 'I still think of it as old Madras. One street may be full of Muslims, and another full of Christians. So many places still have the old charm. Some of these houses are like the ones in Chettinad, with a space in the middle where they dry chillies, and they co-exist with these big Portuguese mansions like Leith Castle. Sadly, the Tamilian houses are all being demolished.'

As she pressed some home-made liqueur chocolates into my hands, she exclaimed, 'I loved teaching. I'm grateful I had two careers, one teaching and the other politics. Everything I have … the pensions I now get … I worked hard for it though I've had tremendous good fortune too. At seventy-eight, I still continue to work for the Anglo-Indian community and women in general. I am happy!'

7

Thinnais and Inner Spaces

'You can write to me at the cage number 190, Calcutta Zoo.'
M Krishnan

A city on any given day presents itself in two different ways. A traveller to this city records her impressions, and indeed reactions, to what she sees on the streets – buildings, people, shops, vendors selling all sorts of wares and the Marina, the large stretch of shell-speckled beige sand that we are so proud of because it is the second longest beach in the world.

And there is the city known to its inhabitants. That city is a web of details. Details relating to locality, one's home, one's neighbours, the shops one frequents, the familiar faces of the shopkeepers, the pulse of the neighbourhood, the many sounds through the day that are the sound of life itself. A spatial web spreads across the city from one's home: the roads leading to school, college, place of work, temples, grocery stores, doctors, hospitals, friends, relatives, jewellery shops, liquor dens, restaurants, shops specializing in certain wares, vegetable markets, pawn-broker's rooms, the beach, the sea and finally roads leading out of the city as well; an idiosyncratic spirograph that one traces day in and day out with some variations.

Much of its essence is not on display on its streets but is lived indoors, with the family. The extended family, with all the many relatives visiting from out of town, forms the basic social network. For some, Chennai is a geographical place that sustains their life; for others, a prison to escape from. The city has a long memory though. Many visiting NRIs have remarked on the pleasure of being recognized by the owner of the local grocery store years after they have left.

In my own personal map of the city, the road most frequented was the central Edward Elliots Road, now called Radhakrishnan Salai, and the destination Perunkulam House.

The earliest friends my father made when he came to Madras as a bachelor were M Krishnan, India's most eminent naturalist and his wife Indumati Krishnan. Their home, Perunkulam House or PH, was a second home to me. In a city where we had no relatives, theirs was the closest I had to a grandparent's home.

Krishnan's father was the renowned Tamil writer and reformer A Madhaviah whose work in the Salt and Abkari Department brought him to Madras, where he remained after he retired prematurely. Leasing land from the Wakf Board for ninety-nine years, in 1922 he had built a white two-storey house with thick walls in pleasingly classic lines, naming it after the village of his ancestors. A 'cottage', set at right angles, housed his printing press, from where he published his magazines *Panchamirtham* and *Tamizhar Nesan*. Just three years later, he passed away at the relatively young age of fifty-three. Krishnan, his youngest child, the eighth and therefore aptly named, was eleven years old at the time.

As an adult, Krishnan would go on to occupy the 'cottage' – empty of the printing machinery – and a newer block of rooms built behind it. In an article titled 'Bird Life in A City', he described what the area surrounding his home was like when he was a child.

There were a few bungalows around, and many groves and fields in between. Our road, or rather the section of it that held our house, was the northern boundary of an oblongish area, the other three sides of which were also closed in by roads. I am tempted to draw a map, but words will do. The tramline and a row of houses formed the eastern edge. The southern edge was more or and less lined with residences, and a new colony (to which we belonged) was coming up on the north – but the west was still wild.

The triangular, south-western half of the oblong was a series of paddy fields, coconut groves and pastures, with only two small churches and a "mutt" to break their continuity. I use the past tense from a regard for accuracy. I live in the house that my father built, and the locality still retains its oblongish shape, but it is chockfull of construction now, built up ruthlessly with just sufficient space between for secondary roads.

In those days I used to wander around with a catapult in my hand and a jack knife in my hip pocket, feeling every inch a settler in a new land. There was a pond on either side of our house and a much larger one on the southern periphery – all these are filled up and built over.

My neighbour's compound was a miniature jungle. In it were mongooses, palm-civets, snakes, tortoises in the pond, even a starry-eyed black buck, though I must confess that it wore a collar. Beyond, further west, were the paddy fields, coconut plantations and scrub which jackals visited after sunset and where the quail were not uncommon after the rains: once, I saw a hare here. It is all concrete and metalled byroads now, and squirrels and rats are about the only wild beasts one can find in it.

Krishnan wrote this article in 1953. My memories of PH date

from the seventies onwards and by then, not only were the surroundings 'all concrete' but it was impossible to imagine that there were ever fields and plantations within memory's distance. Through the day, PTC buses juddered to a halt at the stop right outside the gate, with much screeching of brakes and the shrill conductor's whistle. And in time, Edward Elliots Road was renamed Dr Radhakrishnan Salai after one of its other eminent residents.

PH was one house away from the landmark Rajeshwari Kalyana Mandapam, long considered a lucky place for those who got married there. A *kalyana mandapam* is a self-contained, often sprawling, unit that provides all requirements for a wedding in one place. Rooms for relatives who have travelled from far, rooms for the bride's family, kitchens, vast halls where 500 people can be fed at one sitting, the actual enclosure where the wedding takes place, and a stage for artistes.

Almost every day there was a wedding at Rajeshwari. Standing in the courtyard at PH, one could see streamers of light gaily decorating the side visible to us. The air was filled with loud music that varied from raucous, badly sung film music to the most sublime of Carnatic krithis. Krishnan worked steadily through all this, even though his darkroom and easy chair were the closest to the kalyana mandapam.

The best part, especially for the children in PH, was watching the marriage processions of north Indian families. One heard the band playing long before they neared, and there was time to summon everyone to the gate. The bandsmen wearing all sorts of clashing colours, the liveried men carrying lanterns and lights mounted on tall poles, the march of the drums, all this would go by and then there he was, the bridegroom, a magical figure on a caparisoned horse. If we were lucky, we got to see his face before the veil of flowers swept down as he dismounted. Silks, gold and diamonds, pageantry, familiar tunes from the movies – in the days before television, this was high entertainment that lasted a good half an hour.

To my family, as to many others, attending a wedding at Rajeshwari meant the opportunity of walking up to PH as well.

Standing on the road outside one could look down the driveway to the cottage-like dwelling with a tiled A-roof that sat low on the house. A triangular peak, lower than the main roof, covered the verandah in front.

The view was partly obscured by the spray of mehndi leaves, a fountain of green, now opaque now translucent as the sunlight played on the leaves. A jasmine creeper graced the entrance with its fragrance. The decorative *kolam*, hand-drawn with rice flour, shone on the reddish earth. Half-accepted offering for the ants, it was often smudged as people stepped thoughtlessly on it.

This was Krishnan's home, its tall wooden doors facing north and the road, always open in welcome. The main house had an east-facing entrance, not visible from the road.

The vast area in front of both houses was left untended. Save for a huge neem tree and the lovely green mehndi shrub, the flat ground was open to the sun and rain, and there were many times when one waded through water to reach the porch. Leaves, fallen randomly, lay forlorn on the ground. Sickle shaped on the outer rim, the dry neem leaves were like green paper. To the right of the gate, a solitary ashoka tree stood sentinel.

Krishnan believed that like animals, people also needed a space of their own. You had to take care that you stayed at the perimeter and did not stray into that private space of an animal. Indu and Krishnan respected each other's territory, their different interests and pleasures.

By a curious accident of architecture, Indu's living area was the cottage while Krishnan's area – his room with an attached bathroom built over the kitchen, the darkroom and another room for storage – was located in the newer building behind.

Visitors dropped in at any time of the day. Indu and Krishnan, both warm-hearted, greeted us in their characteristic ways. Indu, in the verandah, by displaying a new sari or talking about the latest film she had seen, and Krishnan, upstairs in his room, by narrating a story from his many travels.

All one saw of the cottage was the roof and the small triangular peak that framed the front door. There was no face to the building, just the mouth of the door alone through which one reached a magical world.

The cottage was low, its roof low and even on the verandah nothing was visible inside except the open door and the dimness inside. In the evening though, the light from Indu's room shone like the heart of the house glowing deep inside.

On either side of the double doors of the cottage was that architectural feature so essential to Tamil homes, the *thinnai*. Placed near the threshold they allow one to offer hospitality to any caller without having to take them inside. Bored with the interior of the house, one can always loll on the thinnai, watching wayfarers. When neighbours or friends gather on the thinnai, it provides the necessary stimulus for gossip.

In PH, they provided expandable and ready seating for all the many guests who came to call on Krishnan, these solid blocks of cement along the length of the wall, with a metal-coloured glaze on top.

It was the best place to lie in summer, the length of cement cool against the spine and sea-breeze like a garment of air billowing around one's body, reading issues of the *Junior Statesman* with Krishnan's grand-daughter, Asha. It was here that Romulus Whitaker, the snake expert brought an innocuous cloth bag that seemed to alter shape every few minutes. When he dipped his hand in and brought out a snake, the crowd on the thinnai dispersed fast. It was here that the neighbour's dog, Johnny, bit Indu's wrist and blood spilled all over the porch. It was seated here that we exclaimed over fine cotton saris brought in tall bundles by itinerant salesmen from Bengal. And when Krishnan was free for a while of his work, he would fold his long limbs into a cane chair and we were in for a wonderful session with the terrific raconteur that he was.

One of the busiest roads in Madras lay outside the gate. The traffic was constant, unrelenting. Sirens sounding when the Chief Minister's car and cavalcade whizzed by. Buses, scooters, autorickshaws, cars, hand-hauled carts – all sorts of vehicles representing the world of commerce, self-interest and grim intent. Those other worlds that existed, so different in ambience from this house, ended with the road. Once inside the gate, all the noise and the bustle receded. Safe on the thinnai, the eyes registered the cars and the buses, their to-and-fro movement as remote, beyond.

The doors, decades old, were big and imposing, almost as tall as the wall. The left half of the door had a big slot for the post. At the back, an enormous box held all the post delivered to Krishnan. A long, slim bolt, like a gun, lay along the top edge of the door. One had to push the right door slightly in order to open the left, when the wood expanded in the rains.

Crossing the threshold of the cottage, one entered a long hall, partitioned into smaller rooms over which the tiled roof floated at a height giving a sense both of space and shelter from the burning light of summer. The first of these was the 'drawing room' though guests were free to tail Indu and Krishnan all over the house, and conversations took place at many different spots. Tall, glass-fronted almirahs held hardbound volumes, and stacks of old newspapers, *The Hindu, The Statesman*, half-read or waiting to be read lined the shelves built into the wall. When television entered our lives in the eighties, then one appeared here as well.

The room furthest inside and its ante-chambers formed Indu's living quarters. A gap between the wall and the sloping roof allowed a ribbon of sky and green trees to run along one side of the room. Breeze, gusts of it from the Bay of Bengal, was as much a presence in the house as people.

Central to the room, and Indu's life, was her puja. Among the many idols, the most precious item was a small naturally shaped stone shivalinga, whose contours matched that of Mount Everest. The tallest figure was a clay image of blue-skinned Krishna leaning against a white cow, a lovely expression on his face. When in time it broke, it proved irreplaceable.

Her bed topped by a mosquito net, mirror and dressing table with a silver-backed comb and brush set, two cupboards, a showcase with many different bric-a-brac and a rosewood bench filled the room. While her expensive silk saris or sentimentally precious ones were locked away in the squat almirah, her everyday cottons were piled neatly on the rocking chair. Indu never needed an iron for her saris. Folded, they were placed under the mattress and came out looking perfectly pressed.

Depending on the vagaries of the sun, the house dimmed and brightened. If the sun played with the clouds, the house sank into gloom. If it dazzled, the house cheered up. Dimness and light were at constant play as one moved about the cottage. When one entered, one's eyes adjusted from the white heat outside to soothing coolness. Inside, light reflected on the black stone of the floor, the slabs gleaming dully. Sometimes, on a wall, a spray of sunlight would ripple like water.

Indeed, there came a time when water flowed right into the house during the monsoon because the main road outside had been tarred repeatedly, raising its height. Indu sloshed about quite calmly, though the water ruined the lower half of the furniture.

I loved Indu's room most of all because of the many, many photographs that hung on the walls, as well as the 'paintings' in embroidery – calendar prints brightened with silk thread, done by Indu's mother, Manorama.

I could spend hours looking at them. Photographs of wildlife taken by Krishnan; of Krishnan when young with a full head of hair and round-rimmed spectacles; their son Harikrishnan as a schoolboy, Indu's friends and relatives – all black and white. And a coloured portrait of Indu as a lovely young bride.

In an era before videos and digital cameras and smart phones, each of these photographs was precious; each held time and a story captive. I only had to point to a black-and white photograph with yellowing edges and Indu would dip in and out of a lake of memories. Her marriage to Krishnan in 1937 was unusual for the times. He twenty-four, she just fifteen. He Tamil Iyer, she Maharashtrian Chitpavan. The birth of her only child Harikrishnan in 1938 ... Years were joined together by a thread created of the moment. Who could tell just which word or which thought would jostle another, dislodging a memory that belonged later or earlier in linear time?

A door at the back of Indu's room led into the courtyard.

Indu had always wanted the typical plant-holding platform, *madam*, built for her tulsi plant. One day Krishnan did just that and the tulsi was installed between her room and the entrance to the kitchen. Though the holder was comparatively new, at dusk when the kolam was drawn brightly in front of it, and the lamp lit and placed in the niche, golden in the oncoming night, the plant became an entity, alive. It was as though there was something eternal and unchanged in the house.

The kitchen was divided by a cupboard, into the cooking and dining spaces. Two small windows set high in the wall and a skylight provided the only natural light near the stove. Open shelving on one side of the wall held the cooking vessels and plates and cutlery. In the years before Krishnan acquired a fridge, a small meat safe kept food cool and safe from ants. Before a square table and chairs were installed, meals were eaten seated cross-legged on a very low wooden plank – *palakais*. The seating was L-shaped then, people taking their place in a row as food was served.

Indu, who was never interested in cooking, was more than happy to let Krishnan take charge of the kitchen. It was not an uncommon sight for visitors to see Krishnan slicing vegetables into precise, symmetric pieces or stirring something over the stove while Indu sat at the table in the kitchen, chattering about this and that, quite secure in the knowledge that the meal Krishnan was about to prepare would be a delicious one.

The bathroom was just that, a room where one bathed, with a sink for washing. The lavatory was Indian-style, in a separate shed outside and away from the kitchen, following the architectural rules of earlier times. When it became necessary for Indu to have the convenience of a western commode indoors so that she would not have to leave her room at night, it caused her a lot of inner conflict for the toilet chamber was separated from her puja by a thin wall.

The courtyard was occupied by the two essential grinding stones – the circular one with a hollow for idli batter, the flat slab for chutneys – and a hip-high sloping one for washing clothes. The electric grinder rendered obsolete the idli grinding stone, and so also the image of the feisty old cook, Shanmugam seated with one leg splayed in front of it, sari drawn up to her knees, rotating the smaller pestle with gusto. In later years, it sat there, heavy, a thing of stone, deprived of its nourishment. Even the pestle lay tilted at an angle of defeat.

One travelled through the day among these structures as from task to task, the rooms in Indu's cottage reserved for the more pleasurable activities – of sleeping, dressing to go out, welcoming friends and communing with her gods.

Krishnan's room upstairs was another continent as it were. A flight of steps led to his easy chair at the very top, in the nook created by two low walls at the landing. Greetings were exchanged as one approached him, climbing the stairs reverentially, so that by the time one had reached him he was ready to plunge into conversation. Krishnan, usually clad in a chequered lungi, was often engrossed in his work but was always ready to put it aside and relax for a while. The only time when it was wise not to disturb him was when he was in his lair, the darkroom, developing prints. When I remember Krishnan, I think of him suspended in the inviting fold of that easy chair, smoking a cigarette.

Depending on what was preoccupying him at the time, he would begin to talk about it. In the course of his discourse, he would meander into other anecdotes and other tales so that by the time he finished the thought he had begun with, he might have linked together topics as diverse as the dismal cricket score, the heavenly sculptures of the Vijayanagara empire, the steep price of carrots and the exquisite *puliodarai* – tamarind rice – that the Parthasarathy temple in Triplicane is famous for. Each time I heard Krishnan speak about his adventures in the jungle or heard his retelling of an amazing experience, I told myself that I would make notes but, to my regret, I never did. The *rasa* was in hearing Krishnan narrate his life story.

To his right, the view of his neighbour's backyard, and to his left, the steps leading down. His paints, an ashtray, cigarettes and match-box laid out in front of him, he worked holding a clipboard. An abiding image is of him leaning forward in that very easy chair, his eye and hand intent on making a pen-and-ink sketch or watercolour drawing that would illustrate an article that he had written.

His other, more formal, workspace was inside his room – desk with a typewriter, negatives meticulously stored and labelled, and a chair in front of the bed. It was bright here, sunlight entering from many windows.

From the height of Krishnan's room, the vast roof of the cottage was visible. The tiles that would have been red once, new and clean, were now dark brown. Here and there, a glimmer of red. Coated with moss, they shone in the rain, as also the rotting mass of leaves that had settled on their surface, impervious to the wind. Standing on the steps, looking at the empire of the roof, the array of tiles, it seemed incredible that Indu lived beneath it, so ancient did it look, vulnerable and brittle with age.

Over the years, Indu who was diabetic and had heart trouble, found it more and more difficult to climb the stairs to

Krishnan's room. Krishnan, who was immersed in his work till the very end of his life, would be busy typing or sketching or writing or listening to Carnatic music. Indu would stand directly below his window and shout whatever she had to say and he would bellow back. They met at lunch, dinner and whenever Krishnan came down.

In their demarcation of 'his' and 'her' space, Indu and Krishnan were far ahead of their times.

Krishnan spent long periods away from home, travelling in the jungles and in wildlife sanctuaries. Once, Indu asked Krishnan for his address in Calcutta where he was going to spend a considerable time. 'You can write to me at the cage number 190, Calcutta Zoo.' When Indu protested, Krishnan attempted to convince her, 'I am going to spend the whole day there, in front of that cage, photographing the macaque. So, that is the best address I can give you.'

The year was 1970. Krishnan was away from Madras, at work in the Corbett Park. Indu received a letter addressed to Krishnan offering him the Padma Shri and wanting to know if he would accept the honour. Indu had no idea when Krishnan would be back. What was she to do? She consulted her neighbour and friend, Rajam Ramaswamy, herself a Padma Shri. Mrs Ramaswamy told her to accept it on his behalf which Indu did. Krishnan was in Lucknow when he heard the announcement over the radio. Indu always believed that by presenting Krishnan with a fait accompli she prevented him from declining the award.

Krishnan had little use for such decorations; they did not define his perception of who he was. He did not attend the ceremony in Delhi. The Padma Shri medal and certificate were sent to him by post. 'You keep it,' he said to Indu, entrusting it to her.

Indu had her own interests, which helped her adjust to his long absences during what she termed their 'long-distance marriage', such as voluntary work for the Consumer Forum. 'I was free to do whatever I wanted, go wherever I wanted. He never questioned me.'

She was addicted to movies and used to visit all the movie theatres in town on her own. Her particular favourites were the Safire/Blue Diamond/Emerald complex, so close to home. Indu had seen the movie *Gone with the Wind* a record eighteen times! Rajesh Khanna was her favourite hero, well into her eighties, and she sniffed into her handkerchief whenever *Aradhana* played on television. Krishnan did not watch movies but Indu had a faithful rickshaw puller, Perumal, who took her on her jaunts to the Mylapore temple or to the theatres.

Krishnan believed that 'the identity of a country depended not so much on its mutable human culture as on its geomorphology, its flora and fauna, its natural basis'.

In his own home, walking down the outer passage that led directly past the cottage to his rooms, one could see that a good part of the grounds was left free for plants to grow as they pleased. That is, there was no cultivated garden but the grown trees formed a canopy beneath the sky. There was a sense of generosity about this use of space, a special quality of disorder.

A big tamarind tree rose above the creepers and wild grass, fruit hanging like fat brown slugs from a stem. As a child, I loved collecting those that had fallen to the ground, breaking the hard chitin to get at the pulp inside, brown sour pulp that pleased even as it stunned the tongue.

The prize woodapple tree was temperamental when it came to yielding fruit. But once harvested, they made the best woodapple chutney I have ever eaten. During a cyclone,

Krishnan bore the sadness of actually seeing it fall when he came down the staircase. It died. Miraculously, another tree grew in its place and Indu called it the son. Its fruit lacked character.

Not much fuss was made of the mango tree here, for the one that Krishnan loved grew in his 'back' neighbour's garden. That *kilimooku* tree chose to bestow all its fruit on Krishnan. He did not even have to stretch to pluck them for the branches heavy with fruit touched the floor of the roof. The rounded mangoes with the hooked 'parrot's beak' lay there, still, as though they had collapsed in the heat. Krishnan could gather them with incredible ease, like flowers from a plant. His eyes, twinkling merrily, he would affirm 'the best mangoes are stolen ones!' Its corollary: the best *avakkai* pickle is made from stolen mangoes!

For Indu, a plant with spiky leaves and bell-shaped yellow flowers, the *thevetia*, was most important. It gave her flowers for her puja gladly day after day, unceasingly. And the ashoka yielded a leaf that she dipped into water and sprinkled on the gods.

Snakes, African snails, frogs, chameleons, worms, insects – there was a thriving wildlife beneath the leaves and creepers that covered the ground.

'Once a stranger came to the door. He was lost,' recounted Indu. 'As he held out the paper with the address, I saw a scorpion near his foot. Had I warned him, he might have stepped back on it. So without saying a word, I held his hand and pulled him in. He was alarmed! Then I pointed at the scorpion and he got even more scared. When I called Krishnan, instead of shooing it away, he got out his camera while the great botanist Dr Swamy, who was visiting, said it was so magnificent he would take it home. Mrs Swamy said, "I am not coming home with you if you do that." Then I asked Krishnan, "Were you not surprised to find a trembling young man?" He replied, "It's hardly an unusual thing to find here!"'

Because the main house stood at angles, and I was so used to rushing straight past it to see Indu and Krishnan, it remained on the periphery of my vision. It was only when visiting this house that I actually looked at its front, at the lines ruled into the wall to the right that appeared like a pattern when photographed, and small square windows set in it. It had a small sloping sunshade of Mangalore tiles, and there was a feeling of solidity about it. A bricked, cemented solidity compared to Indu's cottage where the roof fell low to the ground and the walls were tucked within the overhang of the roof.

For many years the family of Mohammed and Bilquis lived as tenants there. Bilquis, mother to a brood of seven, was known as Khalajaan. Entering the door to Khalajaan's home, one passed beneath a wooden panel hand carved by Krishnan depicting a flight of birds mid-air.

Inside the large hall, the floor was of polished red oxide, a lovely burnished colour. The rooms here had proper walls built up to the roof, as opposed to the cottage. I remember a low platform covered with a thin white-sheeted mattress and lots of round bolsters occupying at least half the room. This was where one found Khalajaan most often. When the time for prayer came, she would spread a rug and offer namaz. It was part of the daily activities of the house, there was no fuss about it.

While one of her daughters, Dr Asfa Zahra was a well-known dermatologist, another, Abida, was a teacher. Indu and Abida were great friends and many of the memorable moments in Indu's life, such as visiting Nepal or praying in a mosque wearing a burkha, were in the company of Abida.

Neighbours, but closer than that by virtue of living in the same enclosed compound, Indu participated in many of their celebrations of births and weddings. Given that children – anybody's, everyone's – are welcome guests in India, I often tagged along.

Later, the entire family shifted to their new home on Lloyds road but the warm ties forged were never broken. And Krishnan's late brother Narayanan's family moved into the main house at PH.

In the way that spaces define a city, and also one's life, Perunkulam House shaped my earliest memories. One unshakeable truth I learnt there, having experienced it, is that a Hindu family and a Muslim family can live together in the same compound amicably, celebrating each other's festive joys.

Indu had always hoped that her death would precede Krishnan's and that she would die a *sumangali* or married woman. That was not to be. Krishnan slipped and fell one morning, breaking his hip joint.

In the hospital run by Christian missionaries, a nun came into his room the day before he was operated on. She was unaware of the eminence of the patient; he was just one of the sick in her charge. She made the sign of the cross over his injured hip and began to pray. Those of us present in the room wondered what Krishnan's reaction would be.

The nun finished praying and assured Krishnan that all would be well. Krishnan, who was unpredictable, to say the least, could be extremely brusque at times. He had no qualms in expressing his dislike or disapproval. I held my breath. Looking up at her from the bed, he said, trying to be genial in spite of the pain, 'I am an atheist, but

I thank you anyway for your prayers.' The nun smiled as she left the room and we relaxed.

Although the broken bone was operated upon successfully, other complications set in and Krishnan passed away on 18 February 1996. A few days earlier, when numerous visitors came to the hospital to enquire about his health, Krishnan remarked with great contentment that he was not a rich man but a man who was rich in friends.

If in 1953 Krishnan observed certain birds no longer visited the city because there were fewer groves and open spaces, by the end of the century it would be safe to say a greater number of birds had fallen off the bird lover's map.

Many homes in Mylapore, especially the old traditional kind near the *mada* streets surrounding the temples, were razed and tall cement blocks obscured the skyline of temple gopuram and coconut palms.

Perunkulam House, it would seem, had been built with its own fate and lifeline. For about a 100 years, Madhaviah had ensured the protection of this land because of the long lease he had taken. The lease running out, Krishnan's family vacated the premises. Indu, as all the other members of the family, had to sort through her possessions acquired over decades, deciding what to keep, for they were going to a much smaller place. I could not bear to go there on the last day, not even to help.

The property was worth crores, space being calculated not only on the floor but also in vertical cubic feet, up in the air. That much unutilized land in central Madras? What a waste!

Months later, the cottage, the main house, Krishnan's private quarters, his darkroom were all razed to the ground. The compound wall remained, enclosing rubble and the shock of empty space. Sunlight filtering through the neem leaves left a filigree of shade on the land beneath one's gaze; a black imprint of blurred shapes on the outside wall. The gateposts still bore the name Perunkulam House.

Many months after that, a squat multi-storey building rose over those acres, swallowing every inch of exposed ground. And perhaps in a metaphor of great meaning, those new offices with plate glass doors and centralized air-conditioning were occupied by Reliance-owned companies.

8

Of Hunger and Riches

*'Why do we use caste surnames at all, especially in birth
certificates? I want to change all that.'*
Sarathbabu Elumalai

Not far away from Krishnan's home, down the same
road, was that flag-bearer of Udupi-style restaurants –
New Woodlands Hotel. Were guests to suddenly descend
on Krishnan leaving him no time to cook, he could always
depend on the inexpensive 'ready meals' from Woodlands,
carried home in giant tiffin carriers.

Established by K Krishna Rao in 1938, Woodlands was
at once an inspirational fairy tale and an example of astute
positioning in terms of location, price and vegetarian fare.
Krishna Rao came to Madras in 1920 as an impoverished,
uneducated boy from Udupi. He worked in various lowly
positions in a hotel in George Town and soon, by dint of sheer
hard work, became manager of a branch. Ten years of experience
at running his own hotel, Udupi Sri Krishna Vilas, on posh
Mount Road, gave him the confidence to take on the much
larger hotel situated in the 'Woodlands' estate in Royapettah.

He made a tremendous success of it and when the lease
was not renewed on the property, he started the 'New'
Woodlands Hotel, which he then took worldwide as part of
a chain (inspiring many clones and spin-offs) that made the
name 'Woodlands' synonymous with 'vegetarian'.

In a city where inflation is assessed by the rising cost of
jasmine flowers and fresh coconut water over the years, the

price of the vegetarian thali at Woodlands served in their Krishna restaurant is my standard measure. Of a style that has become ubiquitous, the furniture here is stolid, lighting dim and the no-frills décor unchanged in decades. And there is great comfort in that.

Just as there is comfort in knowing that when my thali arrives, I will find everything just so. The pulpy *kootu*, sambar, aromatic rasam, the curd-*pachidi*, tamarind-based *kuzhambu*, the dry vegetable *poriyal*, the crisp *appalam*, dessert of the day – *peda* or gulab jamun, the smooth curd individually set in the dish, all ringed around an empty space in the centre, waiting to be mixed with hot rice and golden ghee. The solicitous waiter intent on replenishing my plate even before I have begun eating. And … the coup de grace at the end, when my stomach is close to bursting, the snowy temptation of their famous vanilla ice-cream. Finally, the *beeda*, lightweight version of the more elaborate, syrupy paan, extends the experience long after one has left the premises.

On a trip to America, entrepreneur Krishna Rao was so taken by the trays he found fixed to the sides of cars at McDonald's, he decided he had to introduce them in Madras. In 1962, further down the road, he started the Woodlands Drive-in which, because he had leased it from the Agri-Horticultural Society, was densely filled with rare botanical flora.

Woodlands Drive-in restaurant was quintessentially Madras, in the quiet that prevailed despite being situated near two of the busiest roads, in the delicious idli-sambar that appeared magically on trays appended to the car-window, in the old-world courtesy of its bustling waiters and the fact that it welcomed all, clerk or industrialist. While elsewhere the city sprouted malls and youngsters earned big money overnight at call-centers, inside the Drive-in time was on hold.

My soul was nourished by its peaceful atmosphere, the canopy of green filtering out the brightness of sky, and the aroma of ghee, foot-long dosais and filter coffee. I can visit the Drive-in now only in my memory; a part of the city, like the old Spencers building, that has vanished forever.

On such nostalgia-filled days, I head to Woodlands for a thali.

If there is one food item that instantly captivates newcomers to the city it is the idli. Made of fermented rice and black lentils ground in a certain proportion, the steamed, soft, fluffy idli is the closest thing to serving the moon on a plate. Its blandness makes it versatile – to feed babies or the sick – and the fact that it is relatively inexpensive means that even the poor can afford it. Its cousin, the crisp dosai made of day-old batter, follows in popularity.

In the days before the mixie, intensive labour was required to grind the soaked rice and dal into smooth batter. In any home, it was possible to eat idlis and dosais and chutney only when the cook or maid or mistress spent at least an hour grinding, painstakingly rotating the pestle with her left hand while pushing the rice into the stone mortar with her right.

Remembering this helped me appreciate just how much effort Sarathbabu's mother put into ensuring he got a decent education when she sold idlis off the footpath.

It was the first of the month and flush with her meagre salary of Rs 30, Sarath's mother Deeparamani had brought home a rare treat: 50 gms of 'mixture'. Saving half for later, she filled five paper cones with equal parts, one for each of her children. 'Let's see who makes it last the longest,' she encouraged them. Nine-year-old Sarath, perennially hungry, polished off the gram-flour snack in seconds, hoping his siblings would give him some of theirs. They didn't.

Craving some more, Sarath's eye fell on an ant laboriously carting a tiny vermicelli-like piece across the mud floor of their hut. He relieved the ant of its prize; relished that last speck of food on his tongue. 'No one knew I had done it, but later I felt bad. Stealing from an ant ... that's what the pain of hunger will make you do.'

I studied the thirty-three-year-old seated opposite me in a noisy Café Coffee Day: wavy hair, dazzling teeth and suffering from a sore throat that day. In the ordinary trousers and cotton shirt he wore, in his appearance and unassuming manner, there was nothing to suggest the 'Food King' millionaire he now is. The only clue was the new BMW parked outside. The place itself, one of the many that had sprung up across the city, offered a neutral space for people, mainly youngsters, to meet; away from the public eye. I would have used the word inexpensive as well, but as Sarath's description of poverty unfolded, a story told in single rupees and paise, any expenditure here seemed prodigal.

'I come from a very poor background. My mother knew the value of education. She worked as an ayah in a school, feeding children their mid-day meal scheme. She could have sent me to a government-run corporation school for free, but she chose to send me to an English medium school.'

This decision was to cause both torment to Sarath and lay the foundation of his future success. 'My classmates were all middle class or upper middle class. The food they brought was totally different from mine which was yesterday's rice with today's sambar. I could not share it with them. Just looking at it they would know that it was not good food. They wore new casual-dress to school functions, or on Deepavali and Pongal. My mom never got me a new dress ... My uniform was old and my shoes torn. They did not make fun of me, but they would show off. I felt really bad.' Sarath used the word 'dress' here in the way it has been absorbed into local parlance to mean clothes.

When Deeparamani could not pay the fee of Rs 10 for his LKG classes, she had to shift Sarath to another school, in the first standard. 'As far back as I can remember I always craved recognition. In the new school, when I was six or seven, I scored first marks in a subject. I felt proud, confident and happy. I realized that I did not need to depend on anyone for this feeling. The book, the class, and the teacher … were enough to get recognition. It did not need money. I decided to study, to be the first rank holder in every class.'

Sadly, here too, Deeparamani often could not pay the fees on time. Month after month, little Sarath found himself standing outside the class, subjected to comments and ridicule. 'At first, I was happy. I would whisper, chit-chat with the others who were similarly punished. One day, I decided to overlook the humiliation of standing outside, the pain in the knees, people commenting, and concentrate on the board and the teacher.'

Fees were obligatory; the uniform could be worn threadbare. Sarath had just one single uniform – maroon trousers and chequered shirt – and no other set of clothes. 'Washed over and over, worn daily, it faded and tore. My mother would stitch it up but again it would tear. I'd hide the holes with my books or bag. It had to last two years or more.'

Once, when Sarath was in the third standard, a teacher asked him gently if he would mind wearing her son's old uniform. 'I told myself it is okay to beg for studies. "No problem," I said, accepting it as *bhiksha*. I would think to myself, *I live in a hut, they all live in good bungalows but a hundred years later, we will be old*. In my mind, I would travel to the moon and look down at my hut and the bungalow, finding *both* turned into tiny spots – I made everything relative, so anything that distracted me from my goal became insignificant.'

Listening to Sarath talk, it was clear that his mind had actively engaged with his circumstances, always trying to overcome the negatives.

Even when that mind was dulled by hunger.

'My mother sold idlis in the morning, to earn extra money. The leftover idlis, she would feed us as tiffin, as well as lunch. She cooked a meal for us only in the evenings, and I would *wait* for that.' After his dinner, by the light of the kerosene lamp, Sarath would observe his mother drinking lots of water. 'I thought she really liked water. It was only when I was about twelve years old that I understood she was doing it to fill her stomach.'

That realization was to forever alter his goal in life. 'I thought to myself, *To get food you will steal from an ant. Your mom sacrifices for you. From God's perspective, my mom and I are the same ... but one life is sacrificing for another.* What could I do to help her? I could study well, go to college, get a job, and then tell her not to worry. If I did not study well, all her hard work would be wasted.'

Having found his goal in life, Sarath almost did not get to achieve it. An accident while swimming resulted in the death of his friend Titus while Sarath almost drowned. It had a deep impact on Sarath. 'I felt I now was carrying two lives, not mine alone but my friend's as well. I had to succeed for his sake as well.'

He continued to focus on his studies, challenging himself to do better in each exam. Financial help trickled in, such as the year two teachers paid his annual fees, or the years he got free tuition and a pen, pencil and notebook from the Satya Sai Seva Samiti.

The extent of Sarath's world was his school, and home in a slum in Madipakkam: thatched roof and walls of dry woven coconut leaves demarcating two rooms. 'Even the door was thatched.' The single source of entertainment was the Panchayat-owned black and white television in the locality, which showed movies of MGR on Sundays. Sarath became a life-long fan of the actor and beams when I tell him that he bears some resemblance to him.

Madipakkam was very much on the far outskirts of Madras in the eighties and neglected in terms of development. The sprawling entity of the city did not exist for Sarath. 'In my childhood I never thought I am living in a city. My grandma's home is in north Madras, Kasimedu, near the harbour. Once in a year or two, my mother would take all of us to visit her. On that day, from the bus, I would look at the city pass by – the fifteen-storey LIC building [for decades the tallest in the city, until the nineties], Marina Beach ... There was a house opposite my grandma's house and it was a thrill to climb three floors and see the sea from its roof.'

When he reached the ninth standard, teenager Sarath worked part-time in a leather company, making purses and shoes. 'It is difficult to study when hungry. I constantly felt very tired. My mother reduced the nutrition quotient in the food, less dal, no vegetables, because the prices had risen. I was very thin and bony.'

In the tenth standard, when Sarath would appear for the all-important Boards, the gap between his classmates and him in terms of wealth and conveniences depressed him. 'Then, I imagined their well-lit rooms. They could see everything, the walls, the posters, the people ... distracting them from their textbooks. But having no electricity, I could see only my book in the narrow flare of the kerosene lamp. I learnt to explore the positive in any situation, rather than the negatives.' He earned some money doing book binding, charging less for parents referred to him.

Hunger pursued Sarath in the last two years of school as well. He was older now, his body bigger. 'I had no energy and felt weak. To save energy, I decided not to play for six months. The next six months, I did not do the usual chores for my mother. I made up my mind to speak less than 10 words a day. Within a week I spoke less than 50 words a day, the next week I hit my target. I would count words, 7 words, 3 words. *Oh god, I exceeded by a couple of words.*' He continued this self-imposed austerity for six months. 'It was tough, but a great period for me to understand people, life.'

Never able to wake up early in the morning, Sarath tested himself further. Fearing that the thin blanket made him too comfortable, he decided to sleep on the bare floor in his shorts. Waking up at cold midnight, he would shift to another spot and study for seven hours till dawn. There was no electricity in the hut, nor money to fuel a lamp night-long; he positioned his book in such a way that light from the street lamp fell on it. 'What gave me energy was the thought, *When your mother is able to sacrifice food for you, you can sacrifice sleep for her.*'

His stoic determination resulted in his doing well in the school-leaving Board exam. A friend advised him to join BITS, Pilani; a route to a job. Sarath had never heard of IIT nor for that matter, BITS. Gaining admission to BITS, in itself an achievement, now meant he had to find money for the fees. Astronomical, from his perspective. 'For the first six months, it cost Rs 47,000. It was unimaginable … my mother was only earning Rs 600 a month by then.' Sarathbabu did manage to get a scholarship for Adi Dravidar/Dalits, but it covered only the fees. 'She pawned my sister's jewellery and took a high-interest loan. I thought my problems were over.'

Only, they had just begun.

If his classmates in school were middle-class, 'In BITS they were from an affluent upper-class, English-speaking background, all state rankers. My English was not so good. When they talked about Sidney Sheldon, John Grisham, Pierce Brosnan ... I used to wonder in which class the teacher taught this, maybe I missed the lesson.'

Not used to the concept of treating, Sarath accepted the 'generous' hospitality of his classmates, until he belatedly realized that he would have to reciprocate some day by paying the bill for twenty people. 'I could not spend Rs 100 on a meal. My mom gave me Rs 40 a month for soap, detergent and toothpaste.' He began to make excuses to avoid going out with them. That created other problems. 'If you don't talk to them you don't get tips on exams, tests.' One boy guessed Sarath's predicament and was friendly, though careful not to be seen too often with him.

In the twelfth standard, Sarath had a single pair of pants and two shirts. Though in BITS he had the sudden luxury of three sets of clothes, it did not help that his classmates seemed to have a vast, and expensive, wardrobe. 'Because of this, I skipped a lot of classes in BITS.' Still, he did reasonably well in his exams.

Having no one to guide him, and not knowing exactly what Engineering as a subject meant, Sarath chose Chemical Engineering because he liked Chemistry. Two years passed.

The third year was to be pivotal in moulding a new Sarath, the man he now is. His juniors insisted on voting him in as the co-ordinator. 'I had no idea how to conduct meetings, in English!' Again that old steely determination came to the fore. In the privacy of his room, he began to practise in front of the mirror, getting over his diffidence about speaking in English, as he imagined himself addressing a group of many. Soon, he was comfortable speaking in public.

Just when his goal seemed nearer – he would graduate, get a job and actually hold a pile of cash in his hands – someone suggested that Sarath study at IIM, which would enable him to earn a salary as high as a crore. 'My dream became one crore rupees. I would calculate … every month I would earn eight lakhs thirty thousand, I would save some three or four lakhs and buy a car – in seven months I would buy seven cars, and keep it outside my hut – passers-by would see it and realize that my mom's hard work had paid off!'

But destiny had other ideas for Sarath.

Training in Dhanbad, Jharkand a few months before he passed out of BITS Pilani, he read with dismay in a newspaper that nearly 30 per cent of India's population goes to bed hungry.

'I could not sleep trying to figure out what the solution could be and I realized that we need entrepreneurs who can provide quality jobs to thousands of people, especially those from the needy sections of the society.

I thought to myself that if we had a 100 entrepreneurs and each of them could create 1,00,000 jobs, then one entrepreneur would end up supporting 5,00,000 people, if each family had five members.'

The interesting thing about Sarath, I was soon to learn, is his delight in numbers. Any idea or problem, or solution, when quantified in dizzying numbers such as crores, becomes easy for Sarath to grapple with. 'Finding that one entrepreneur in 1,00,00,000 people seemed possible and I thought that I should lead by example. If my education was only going to help me live and eat and die, it was mere selfishness. If my mother's sacrifice had to have real meaning, I had to do good to society.'

While he was envisioning this, there was hard reality to be faced. On graduating from BITS, Pilani, he had a debt of Rs 1.5 lakhs. He needed a job. When everyone on campus got placed, Sarath did not. 'At every interview I would frankly say, "I will work only two years with you because I am going to start my own company." My friends and classmates stopped talking to me because now they belonged to a different league, with posh jobs in multinationals.' He made up his mind to race ahead of them. (Seven years later, when BITS, Pilani named their most distinguished alumni, Sarathbabu Elumalai was one of thirty.)

Eventually, Sarath did get a job at Polaris Software, and studied alongside for the CAT exam required to get into IIM. The dream of entering IIM had been tweaked, not to get him the salary of Rs 100,00,000 – seven zeroes! – but to learn management skills, so that he could start his own company and help the estimated five lakh people.

'I cleared CAT the fourth time, gained entrance to all six IIMs and chose to study at Ahmedabad in 2004.' By now, with work experience behind him and much improved English, Sarath could blend in with the students at IIM-A. 'They did not know about my background. I never shared my dream ... They saw me as someone at the same level, from BITS and Polaris.'

Two years later, it was placement time again. 'All the hard work and studying would pay off now, with a good job and fantastic pay packages. Ahead of me, one door led to a job, a comfortable life, and a suitcase full of money, another revealed a cave that was dark, and full of spiders and thorns but at the back of which I could see my dream world shimmering.'

Taking a long eight-kilometre walk across the campus, Sarath tried to arrive at a decision. 'I understood that the

IIM-A certificate had a value only because I was alive. And after twenty-seven years of struggle with no money, all I had was these two degree certificates with me. The more years I spent in a job saving money and building assets meant that for those many years I could not impact a needy person's life directly. Then I told myself: *Money challenged you for so many years, now you challenge it.* It was a great moment for me, when I decided to tell money – *I do not need you.*'

The next morning, at the placements session, 'Around me all the students were talking about job profiles, state, city, salaries. I told them I was not going to accept any of the jobs. I had zero income. No proper bank balance, nothing. Just Rs 2,000 in hand. Later, I took my mother to the convocation and revealed my plans in public.'

That was the year Sarath became famous. Newspapers across India carried the story of his impractical, even foolhardy, decision.

On April 1, perhaps a mocking nod to April Fool's Day, 'I incorporated my catering services company, Food King, in Ahmedabad.' The co-founder of Infosys, NR Narayana Murthy inaugurated it. 'My first, tiny order was to supply eighty teas and twenty coffees twice a day to a company called System Plus.' While the managers who hired him felt embarrassed they were giving such a small order to an IIM graduate, Sarath was thrilled. Now when other companies asked him, he could say he had work experience.

'I was not making much money. You can *start* a company with Rs 2,000 but you cannot run it. I took loans from friends and began to incur losses.'

In December 2006, Sarath attended an alumni event in Mumbai, hopeful of getting a big contract. The meeting went on till late; he did not get the contract; missed his train; had only Rs 200 in hand and was asked to leave the platform by policemen. 'After two hours, I went back inside the station, got a refund and so was able to buy a new ticket. The remaining money was just enough to buy a samosa and have tea. A kind man gave me a newspaper to spread and I slept on the platform!'

'That night, I did wonder if I had made the wrong decision in life. But, even at that low point, I thought about improving the lives of all the others on the platform rather than pitying myself, an IIM-A graduate, for sleeping there. I decided not to give up, but to streamline my company's procedures.'

Back in Ahmedabad, 'I did not take a day off. Not many people know this … I slept on the lawns of IIM-A. From 3 a.m. to 6 a.m. my body would be resting but my mind was churning. All my batchmates had gone, I was the only person on campus. I felt really alone. A dream is one thing, running a company another. I made a lot of changes, saved lots of money, arrested losses.'

Within six months, his luck changed. He got a contract from BITS, Pilani. 'I started making money, repaid my debts. Had a vacation, the first break in my life, and went back to work.' Three years later, his turnover was Rs 7.5 crore.

What changes did that bring in Sarath's life?

'I *do not* waste money. I buy what I require for my work, still stay in my hut. Even now, I don't have many clothes, and do not have an extravagant lifestyle.'

And it was to see the place where he grew up that I gladly accepted Sarath's invitation to visit his home.

Much has changed since Sarath's childhood. Madipakkam is now well connected to central Chennai, indeed is integrated in many ways since a new bypass has come up that links it with other suburbs further south and west.

In Sarath's neighbourhood, of narrow streets and garbage piled high, there has been some degree of prosperity – cement has replaced thatch, the huts are houses now, connected to television and electric cables – but he also rues the appearance of a greater degree of materialism. As I entered his gate, there were cocks crowing in the background. Sarath's old jeep, beneath a mango tree that lends its shade to the front yard, lay splattered with bird-droppings. The BMW was held safe in a newly constructed garage.

He has travelled the world, but what Madras means to him is the fragrance of jasmines sold outside the temple near his home, the distinctive sound of an autorickshaw, the tinkling-bell announcing the *son-papdi* cart, and hero Kamal Haasan for that role in the film *Nayakan,* where he is the protector and benefactor of his people.

Sarath's own home has acquired brick walls and a solid wooden door. The thatched roof is low; the rooms small. What is spacious is the kitchen, clean, tidy, where Deeparamani still presides.

In her appearance too, a thin frame and greying hair, there was nothing to suggest the recent years of prosperity. She wore some gold, but was not encased in it. Sarath was protective of her. 'My mother has really suffered. Father left us early and lived with his second wife and family. My younger brother died when he was in the tenth. Later, my elder brother also died.'

Apart from taking her all the way to Ahmedabad for his convocation, Sarath has frequently mentioned his mother in interviews and loves it when she is honoured as well – such as the time Sri Krishna Sweets felicitated the mothers of several distinguished people, including Deeparamani.

While his mother was busy cooking, Sarath and I got back to talking about his life.

Sarath continued to explain his attitude to wealth. 'I never want to have the money part overwhelm me. I try to be distanced from it mentally, so I am free. We have other properties but I do want to build a bigger home ... maybe I will just get some land behind my home and build on it.' There is a dreamlike element to it, 'I had a very hard life but the rarest of good luck too. Seems like it was all planned for me. Like a pre-recorded life is playing.'

The chamber leading off the main room where we were seated was lined with cement shelves. And on each of those shelves were crammed the many awards, plaques and momentos Sarath has won ever since he started Food King. He was given the Pepsi MTV Youth Icon Award 2008 and in 2011, the CNN IBN Young Indian Leader Award. 'When I get awards, it is one more arrow in my quiver. The kind of work that I do needs lots of strength and support.'

In 2009, Sarath was in the news for other reasons. He had decided to contest the Lok Sabha elections.

This unexpected turn in his life came about when the person next to him on the podium, at a function honouring both of them, talked about how his friend had a Rs 1,500 crore project planned that would only see fruition if a bribe of Rs 500 crore were paid to a certain politician.

Sarath's brain began working the numbers. He could get Rs 500 crore if ten lakh people gave him Rs 5,000 each. With just one of those contributions of Rs 5,000 he could educate, feed and clothe one child. Ten lakh children could be helped with that bribe amount. If ten ministers were each getting such a bribe, from ten such projects, then 1 crore children could be fed for ten years with all that money. Instead, *one* man swallowed all that money for himself.

'These people will not change. The only way is to have new people in the system and replace them. I studied the way our constitution works. In a population of 1.2 billion people, only 7,000 are required to represent the people in Parliament. Can we not find 7,000 good people in this vast country of ours? We keep saying politics is dirty, and after 20-30 years we will say the same thing. There has to be a turnaround. I thought to myself, *It is dirty. No problem, I will clean it.*'

In 2009, Sarathbabu Elumalai decided to contest the Lok Sabha elections. 'I focus on the things I want to achieve: I *am* going to change the world. I never think that things are so fixed that they cannot be changed. We have to make a start.'

There was much learning and much disappointment that was to come his way. The first assumption everyone made was that he was joining politics to make money.

'I told them, "If I had wanted to earn more money ... I have brains, I have a business. When I was in dire need of money I spurned money. So I have not come into politics for money."'

Sarath soon understood that, 'though politicians say they want the youth to join politics, unless it is someone from their own family, they do not encourage newcomers. I thought not many educated people are willing to come into politics but actually politicians don't want people like us to get into it. The party doors are closed. Either you quit or become an independent.' Sarath filed his papers as an independent candidate.

Then he came up against the money-factor, and set patterns of voting. Irrespective of which faction, candidates 'give money. Hard cash. A 1000 rupee note. If they cover 25 per cent of the electorate with money, and get 70 per cent votes, they are set. They are investing their money, to get it back once they win.' That automatically required deep pockets and a huge budget. Sarath stuck to the rules. 'We spent Rs 7 to 8 lakhs on the campaign. The constitution allows Rs 25 lakhs, we spent less.'

Disappointingly, the very slum where he grew up did not give its entire vote to him. 'Even in my area, if they are for a certain party, they will not budge. Makes you realize that the big parties have loyal people. If they have benefited, they continue to vote for them. If you go as an independent and think of winning, you don't stand much of a chance. Everyone thinks an independent cannot win, so they don't vote for a candidate who will lose.'

After campaigning for twenty days, Sarath got 15,890 votes. 'Only.'

Many of Sarath's volunteer campaigners were demotivated. Three months of their lives had been lost to the general elections. 'But I am still in this fight. I think the Lok Sabha is impossible to win, unless I spend Rs 2 or 3 crores which is not a good example.' Although disappointed, he stood for the Legislative Assemby elections in 2011. 'We spent about Rs 8 or 9 lakhs while other candidates were spending in crores.'

Sarath actively campaigned for the local election with one hundred volunteers, visiting 25,000 homes, 'in Velachery, Thiruvanmiyur, Adyar, Taramani, Besant Nagar. I thought if there are four people in a home, we reach 1 lakh people this way. If all of them talk to their neighbours and relatives, we would reach many more people. But out of the 2.5 lakh votes we hoped for, we got 7,500 votes from the middle and upper middle class. Though we did not win, I am confident of winning the next time. In all the elections I've fought, I did not use money as a factor. It would only demonstrate that money makes you win, which would discourage youngsters. They do not have money.'

The same year, Sarath stood for Mayor but did not win there either. If there is one thing that upsets him most of all, it is that 'when I look around, political leaders use caste to their political advantage, making different castes their vote base. Why do we use caste surnames at all, especially in birth certificates? I want to change all that. In my own company, Food King, I assess the attitude of the person and their need, not their caste, and I try to help them.

'Education is the only way to abolish caste and connect people. This is important. Education helped me because I went to IIM-A and BITS. I faced economic disparity but not caste bias. Some of my close friends are Muslims and Iyers.'

For Sarath, his social work is not divorced from his political aspirations. He travels to many places, big cities and remote areas alike, to motivate students by his example. 'I have addressed many youth in schools and colleges, and have inspired many young entrepreneurs in the past five years.' Many of these people who might otherwise have remained unknown to Sarath have found him online and told him about his impact on their lives. 'I am happy the time I spent talking to them did not go waste.'

He has a new dream now. 'My mission is to see a Hunger Free India. Whatever work I do should be aligned to this: entrepreneurship, mentorship, political involvement, helping educate children, giving food to people, all my work should concentrate on this dream. I want October 10 to be Hunger Free Day. On this day, I feed 10,000 people.'

The boy who grew up unacquainted with the rest of Madras, now has over 10,000 friends in the city. 'I have interacted with people from all levels. I can talk to anyone, I have a bandwidth that no one has. That is my strength.'

Deeparamani served lunch. The plump white rice had just been made, and so had the dal-rich sambar. My fingers did a jig over the scalding food, trying to mix the rice and sambar. She had also cooked tender green leaves off the drumstick tree in the backyard. It was a simple meal and delicious; I realized how much I had taken for granted, as a child, certain edibles such as ghee and curd both in my home and that of others.

As I left Sarath's home, I acknowledged to myself that he had just made friend Number 10,001 in the city.

9

Reaching for the Stars

'Auto drivers in Besant Nagar have a sangam and I belong to them.'
Vikram

In a city that worships its film stars, literally – temples have been built for MG Ramachandran and Khushboo, fans of Rajinikant and Kamal Haasan routinely perform arati, break coconuts and bathe posters of their latest releases with megalitres of milk in raucous celebration, people have voted artistes from the world of films such as MGR, Karunanidhi and Jayalalitha to power – to become a film star is perhaps the dream of its millions. Not everyone achieves that dream. Yet, when they do, as did actor Vikram, their relationship with the city changes forever.

Adored by fans, mobbed by crowds, it can mean that many ordinary things such as a visit to the nearby beach can become impossible. I met Vikram to talk to him about the spaces in the city, to ask whether he can freely access certain places, do certain things. Or, has the price of fame been the restriction of free movement?

It was through the songs of his films that I first encountered Vikram. Immersed in writing a novel, I was lost to the world. I had a vague idea of the latest movie hits and had not been to see a movie in a while. My son, a madly energetic eight-year-old then, raced home from his best friend's house singing Tamil songs, something he had a disinterest in until then, and demanded that we buy the cassette. On and on, in a loop,

I heard those songs from *Saamy*, in 2003, one of his many successful and acclaimed films in the early part of the decade – *Dhill*, *Gemini*, *Kasi*, *Dhool*, *Pithamagan*.

Still lost in that creative haze, I was not at all curious about the actors in the film. I liked the songs immensely, though, and soon my son and I would sing along on every car ride. Once, stuck behind an MTC bus, I found myself staring into the eyes of a hero in close-up on a film poster. Wearing a yellow shirt, the first two buttons undone, the man's eyes were magnetic. He stared right back at me.

Some seven years later, doing a triceps pushdown at the gym, a gentleman suggested I ought to hold the bar in a certain way. I glanced sideways at him and back, concentrating on the muscle. Those eyes. I had seen them before somewhere. Wanting to look again, I turned. He was gone.

Later in the gym, in the way details of people are offered easily, I learnt that he was Vikram. Superstar.

In a place filled with mirrors, silver images of Vikram appeared all over the gym room when he worked out – refracted, fractured, multiplied endlessly. Walking on the treadmill side by side with him, it was often easier to talk into the mirror to his reflection there.

The man himself neither broadcast his appearance nor was aloof. Joking with the gym assistants, complimenting them on their ripped look, working with his own trainers, calling out to his friends across the room, Vikram was accessible to all. Most respected the privilege and never asked him for autographs or photographs.

The rare times a newcomer or visitor to the gym did, he obliged but one was displeased on his behalf. 'I shun types who treat me like a hero. I hate cinema talk here, I avoid such people,' he told me.

Clearly the gym was a place where he could be himself – an ordinary guy who did extraordinary things with his body, honing that instrument through exercise and with complete dedication.

In the time it took to talk to him about his life, sitting across a table in the gym, he greeted visitors who clearly could not believe their eyes, involved his trainers in the conversation, and gave advice to a girl on the perennial question of weight-versus-inch loss.

If the city was a place where he could not do certain things like jog or run in the open, the gym offered him a safe environment.

'Guys from boarding school such as me are loners, you keep to yourself, need to have your own space. I too had my own space but when I became an actor I realized that if you put a wall around yourself, no one can get in, and you too can't get out. Which is why I decided to visit the gym for workouts. I'm comfortable here.

'More than anything, the alpha male thing happens in the gym, at many levels though ours is tame that way. I make it clear I am not a hero, I am not an actor here, I am Vikram. Just treat me as normal.

'I'm either at the gym or home. Gym, home or working. You won't find me anywhere else,' revealed Vikram. And in a day, there might be five visits to the gym such as for his blockbuster film *Kandasamy* or twice such as now, when he is working on his look for the film *I*.

Known for his ability to change his body to suit a role, so that he is inhabiting the body of the character, not just emoting face up or relying on disguise, Vikram spent most of 2013 undergoing tremendous weight loss.

Nothing else, not even his acting, can command more empathy and exasperation than the sight of a rich man starving himself voluntarily for a role. While he joked about eating 'green goop' and wanting to lick the remnants of the scanty portion stuck to the dish, those in the gym watching him gradually get thinner and thinner felt sorry for him, certain that such extremes weren't necessary. But not Vikram.

'Already I have lost eleven kilos. I eat ten mini meals. After two hours juice, then two hours later lunch. As I lost weight, I reached my peak and looked good. Then I looked tired. Everyone said, 'What are you doing? Why? But why?' I have to lose the muscle, lose another ten kilos. The next two weeks I will look sick and then after that like a beggar. This is what I am doing for the role. I cannot do it any other way. It is not so much conviction, but that I would not be able to sleep if I could not do it this way.

'Every film of mine I have done something. For *Raajapaatai*, I put on size and weight. In *Bhima* I was a fighter, so I worked out and looked like a thug. For *Dhill*, I ate twenty-five egg whites and a whole chicken every day to bulk up. In *Saamy*,' where he played a cop, 'I put on muscle and a paunch.'

It was time for his micro meal, and he opened a container with what looked like thin strips of vegetables doused in soya or oyster sauce. For a while, he ate that tiny portion with full concentration and relish.

It is clear that Vikram's standards are set far higher than what his fans or the film industry would be content with.

'I am not doing it on a Tamil film scale. I am trying to do it on an international scale. People should appreciate what you have done. I want people to look at my films after ten years and say "Wow! What a body of work!"'

And yet, if there is any frustration, it is about his fans and the industry taking it for granted that he will deliver whatever the role demands in any movie of his.

'People think *Vikram no, he can do it*. If someone does far less, they say, "Wow!" but they think it is easy for me to do all the things I do.'

And popping the last strip of vegetable into his mouth, he declared, 'Next film I am going to be muscular.' No more starving, thankfully.

To his friends, Vikram is Kenny.

Born John Victor Kennedy Vinod Raj in Madras, Kenny studied at Montfort, a residential school in the hill station Yercaud. So for all twelve years of his basic education, Kenny lived away from Madras.

'Whenever I came back from hostel, my parents,' mother Rajeshwari and father Vinod Raj 'kept me at home in Chennai. Basically, I was very shy, would not play much with the other kids. So like a jailbird, I led a cloistered life, would stay at home and then go back to school.'

Completing school, he returned to join Loyola College, but even then 'I had not seen much of the city. We stayed at Lloyds colony, so I knew Lloyds road, CIT Nagar, the lake area.' In fact, he was most unlike his friends in college. 'The first thing a guy gets to know in college is where the girls' colleges are. But I did not know. In the second year, I asked this one guy, 'What is this place?' He said, 'Don't bluff. This is Women's Christian College.' I honestly did not know about WCC. And while I had heard of Stella Maris, I did not even know where it was. So lame! Five years later when I went to drop my sister there, that's when I knew this is Stella Maris College. So imagine how much of Chennai I knew!'

In 1986, his last year of college, Kenny met with an accident that was to change his life radically.

'I was riding pillion. And the guy who was driving the bike was a classmate. Actually, it was a twist of fate ... someone else was supposed to go on the bike but at the last minute he went off with a girl in a car.'

As soon as they took off, Kenny was alarmed to see that the rider was resting his leg on the crashguard even while piling on speed. 'I said, "What are you doing??? Put your leg down!"' Simultaneously, Kenny saw a lorry approaching fast. 'He could not brake. He accelerated instead and we hit the lorry.'

The accident resulted in Kenny's right leg being fractured and damaged to the point that the doctors said he would not walk again. Far from being free to explore the city, Kenny spent his last year of college indoors, bedridden. The one responsible for the accident escaped unhurt. 'Nothing happened to him but I got jacked for life.'

For the next three years, Kenny underwent prolonged treatment at Vijaya Hospital which included twenty-three operations.

While all of this was terrible enough for a twenty-year-old to cope with, what made it worse was that Kenny had dreamt of being an actor from the time in school when he was on stage and heard the sound of applause, rousing applause for him.

'Even back then, when I did other plays, I did not want to do, say, Caesar, but Brutus or Cassius. I would search for roles and characters where the person was interesting, or weird roles which required performance. An actor always wants a bigger audience. Suddenly in the ninth standard, I discovered there is something called cinema. I was mad about acting. My uncle was an actor, as was my dad, so I never thought it was tough to become one. I did think my uncle would help me, but no, I did it on my own. I never thought *I want to be an actor*. I knew I *am* going to become an actor. I will. I am.'

An actor who could not walk? That was not an option.

He brought his willpower to bear.

'When I was in hospital I used to do weights. My legs were *thin* like sticks, I had to have traction. So to build my torso and upper body, I would do dumbbells, and then,' lying flat on his bed, 'benchpress with the food trolley,' lowering it to his chest and raising it in the air. Soon the doctors started bringing patients by, believing Kenny's example would motivate them. 'They would say, "Show your biceps. Show your legs." Then turning to the patient, "See! You have only a broken hand."'

Kenny credits his mother for his attitude. She never thought anything was impossible, and when it came to her son, *nothing* was impossible. There was always a way.

Not only had the accident deprived Kenny of mobility but it had shrunk his horizons. Outside, people in the city went about their daily lives. But his world was now the size of that hospital room – a metal bed, doctors, nurses, a diet of medicines – where distances were rearranged. Inches, yards, feet … the distance from his bed to the door was measured in time. How long would it take him to walk on his crutches to the door?

'Initially, I was okay. Then it got bad. There was no chance of me coming out.' That was the only time Kenny's determination wavered. Maybe the self-knowledge he had about his future needed to be altered in its details. Fame would come, but as 'a singer. Until then I did not sing, but my brother did. I thought *If he can sing, so can I.*'

Around the same time, Kenny watched the movie *Mayuri* about a dancer who loses her leg in an accident and continues to dance with a false one. 'I told my mother, "Cut my leg, put a false leg then I can do a scene." She slapped me, started screaming at me.' For his mother, who had spent hours by his bedside consulting with doctor after doctor, fighting for him, *with* him, this would have seemed like giving up.

Not an option.

When he met his future wife, Shailaja, who was planning to do a PhD in Psychology, 'I was on crutches. She asked me "What do you do?" in the usual way of introductions. I replied, "I am not doing anything now ... but I am going to become a big star. I am going to have these many cars, these many houses." She thought I had delusions of grandeur. I could not even straighten my leg.'

The time came when he was no longer confined to his bed but he was on crutches. He still could not walk on his own, without support. That would take another year. 'I slowly got stronger. I did exercises on my own.'

Kenny got a job at Lintas, the advertising agency, as a trainee. His stipend was Rs 750. 'I would take a bus, go by auto, everywhere, on my crutches. I went to Connemara to use the swimming pool.' All the chest and arm-building exercises came in useful. 'I could not walk but I could swim faster than the coach there!' He also managed to complete his degree.

As he spoke, my mind went back to the first film of Vikram's that I had actually seen in the theatre, the recent *Raavan*. There is a scene where he runs across a rope bridge suspended high up in the air. It is a long bridge and he runs for a quite a while. I had seen a man running who thought he might never walk. It was no illusion; it was real. In my own head, I had to reassess so many things, offering him a mental salute for one.

When he did throw away the crutches, his primary doctor's reaction was gratifying. 'He was shocked! "Kenny, you are walking! You are an actor!"' Despite his elation, the doctor prescribed caution. 'He said, "No, you should not run. You should not jump. No stunts!" But acting *is* about this. Fifteen years ago he told me, "You have the knees of a seventy-five-year-old." It took me all my will power to get where I am today. To *walk*.'

Having watched Vikram in the gym going through his rigorous workout, lifting weights that looked like gigantic tyres, I knew he had focus and determination, but they were raised to an altogether different level when one considers what he had overcome. 'It tells me you have mental strength of an enormous kind,' I could not help commenting.

Kenny nodded. 'It made me very resilient.'

Finally, adopting the screen name Vikram, 'I got into movies. I struggled and struggled. Practising acting with my friends, going for *silambam*,' a form of martial arts using sticks, 'and dance classes, and also learning to walk all over again. I got small movies, then another, then another.'

The first was *En Kadhal Kanmani* in 1990. It did not do well. The second was *Thanthu Vitten Ennai* a year later. It did not make him a star either. He made several other movies, some with directors who had earlier delivered hits. Each time, Vikram thought '*This movie will be my break.*'

By 1994, Shailaja and he were married. 'My parents, wife, were all supportive. My father-in-law helped us a lot.'

He gave Vikram a Maruti car. 'Very sweet of him, it was the first car I owned.' But a car required petrol, petrol cost money, and Vikram had no money. 'I had to manage *with* air-conditioning, on 100 bucks a day, or the petrol would finish. If Mani Ratnam called, I'd want to be fresh when I went to see him. I would drive a little with it on, then switch it off. Do stuff like that!'

Things did not get better even though Vikram made enough movies to be recognized on the streets. He still had not hit big time and his income was barely adequate.

'My dad had an Omni. I would always keep it filled with just five litres. After I became an actor, it would always run out of petrol and I would have to push it to the petrol pump. It's funny, when you want to be recognized, say in an airport where you need a ticket in a hurry, people look blankly at you. But on the road, everybody would recognize me when I was pushing the car. "Sir, Vikram Sir ... *maatintingala*? Stuck? *Yenna thalaiva, padam illaiya*? What boss ... No film on hand?"'

It was galling.

By now Vikram had done films in Malayalam as well as Telugu. He had dubbed for other actors, he had directed a telefilm. He was known, but he was not a star. Perhaps his wife's assessment was right. Perhaps he had delusions about being able to succeed as an actor.

'It went on and on and on,' for nine years. 'The hope that it will be this movie, the hit.' He acted in twenty-two movies in three languages, and all twenty-two of them sank.

Then came a script that was to give Vikram the prefix 'Chiyaan' (meaning a rowdy) and the title to starhood – for the movie *Sethu*. Life would be defined in terms of before and after.

'The struggle was before I got into movies and before Sethu. Bala,' the director, 'said, "Do not do anything else because this movie will come out in all languages." For two years I did not do any other work. Even Sethu took a long time and did not get completed after two years for lack of money.'

In fact, Bala himself had struggled as much as Vikram to make a mark in the film industry. Both the director's and actor's hopes were pinned on this movie. But it had a very stark story, with a sad end, not the usual happy fare. A college rowdy falls in love with a girl. Just when things start to go well between them, tragedy strikes and he suffers a brain injury. Admitted into a mental asylum, his head shaven and face emaciated, Vikram in the last part of the film is unrecognizable from the first half, so completely does he give himself over to the character and the situation. It was an unlikely vehicle for a mass hit.

And to achieve that look, Vikram survived on egg whites, beetroot and carrot juice for a month, apart from shaving his head. That was at the end of a long process where he lost 16 kilos.

First, money ran out and the film was almost abandoned. Then money was accumulated in small amounts and parts of the film made. But when it was ready, no one was interested in distributing it because it was off the beaten track. Ultimately, after Vikram held screening after private screening to get distributors interested, it did get shown in the movie theatres.

'Then it happened,' says Vikram simply.

People came out wiping tears from their faces, disturbed and moved to the core; the low-budget film was a hit and Vikram a star.

Vikram would compare it with the time in school when ten days before the play *The Doctor In Spite Of Himself*, 'a fantastic comedy, the boy playing the hero got chicken pox. I knew all the dialogues so they reluctantly chose me. It is about a woodcutter and the way he goes about being a doctor is hilarious. It was a huge hit and they had a write up saying 'A Star is Born'. Ten years I struggled and no one knew I could act. Then Sethu happened and I got the same headline. *A Star is Born.*'

With other hits, and films offering him the opportunity to play a variety of roles, Kenny did get the many cars and houses he had dreamt of. He told his wife, 'See I did it. I never told you I was going to get a helicopter or a jet. I didn't say that. Just the cars, the houses.'

On many a day, I've seen some of the cars owned by Vikram, his Porsche 911, his silver Audi R8 among others, parked by him on one side of the tree-lined avenue near the gym. Invariably, in his absence, his car attracts a cluster of drivers exclaiming over it. Proximity to his car is just one step away from a chance of seeing him in person. One by one, they leave when their 'owner' comes out of the gym.

Because it is in a quiet neighbourhood, there is no crowd around the car. Vikram can slip into the gym without being mobbed. 'I come here only because of parking. And the people in the gym. I love to drive if it is close by, but if I am shooting and have to go anywhere across Mount Road,' where it is crowded, 'I get a car and driver.'

The irony, of course, is that the traffic and the state of the roads do not allow one to achieve the sort of speed and smoothness of ride the cars are built for. But Vikram says, 'It is not about speed. I came into movies because I wanted good cars. I was never going to be a cricketer! I am a very safe driver. Once I did 130 kmph in the Audi near the Crocodile Bank,' on the scenic and beautifully smooth East Coast Road. 'The maximum I go to is usually a 100 kmph.'

Vikram does not hold back while talking about the improvements required in the city. In all of our conversation, this is the most I have seen him impassioned. 'Everyone would like to say "*My* city, *my* country, I am proud of Chennai". I'm definitely proud of it … only because my folks and friends are here. But I am ashamed of everyone's callousness on the roads, the way we pollute, throw things around, the way we spit, the way we cross lanes, the hustling and bustling and jostling. It pains me. We could make the roads broader. In London, they have narrow roads but they have order, double-decker buses plying on both sides … we don't need six lanes for that. We've got the worst roads. It pains me that we live in the city and cannot do anything about it.'

In terms of public service, 'You put yourself out there and everyone says you are a fool. When we go abroad, we stick to the rules, we change. But when we return we go back to dumping things. After *Anniyan,*' where his performance of a vigilante with multiple personality disorder won him the Filmfare South Best Actor award, 'I don't do that anymore. If you look inside my pockets, I'll have rubbish. Whatever I want to throw away, I wait to find a dustbin.'

It was clear he cares about the city enough to want it to improve. 'Thailand is teeming with tourists because of the way they have promoted tourism. Chennai is a wonderful city, look at the temples, our food, we have so much, even Kerala is able to capitalize on what they have but not us. We need to change. It will happen after generations, if you ask me.'

As for Kodambakkam, for long the geographical hub of all things cinema in Madras, Vikram comments on the fact that it has changed radically. 'None of the film studios exist. May be one or two. Most of them have given way to multiplexes and apartments.' At the same time, 'it is a place where at least three people in a house work in the movie industry. Junior artistes, cinematographers, fighters, dancers … Most assistant directors come from around Madurai though. I don't know why. There's no one from Chennai like a Mani Ratnam or Gautham Menon.'

Recently, Vikram chose the sea-facing Besant Nagar in which to live, building a house there.

Echoing Sivakami's impression on venturing into Adyar, Vikram described the first time he came to Besant Nagar. 'We reached the Ayyappan temple past San Thome. Until there I was happy but when the driver said we are going to Besant Nagar, and I felt we were going *so* far away. Then I fell in love with Shaila and would come here often. It is like an island. The road ends at Besant Nagar, you do not pass through. The only drawback is that on Sundays there is usually a procession or festival and everyone is heading here, crowding the roads.'

Clearly, Vikram has a strong fan base in his own neighbourhood. When the People's University of Milan conferred an honorary doctorate on him in 2011, posters of Dr Vikram in a gown and cap appeared on all the inner roads.

Mainly, the auto drivers in the locality are delighted. A larger than life figure has stepped out of the screen and is living in their midst. Vinyl banners of Vikram and metal boards with his face painted on it are a common sight in Besant Nagar, especially at the auto stands. It is a bit dislocating, to drive past his face pasted on various surfaces – walls, electricity junction-boxes, shop shutters – and then see him in the gym at some point in the day. It points to the mythic space he occupies; people may not be able to see him in person but are surrounded by his images, static and moving. In that sense, he populates the city with a multiplicity of selves, looks, roles.

'Auto drivers have a collective, a *sangam*, and they want to identify with someone. I belong to Besant Nagar so I belong to them. I love going by autos. I would love to take a bus but can't.'

And it was now that I got an answer to the question I had begun with. Did stardom curtail his movements? Well, Vikram does not allow it to.

'I do the most normal things. I go out as much as I can, pick up DVDs, flowers. I watch almost every movie in the theatre.'

When I expressed surprise, Vikram showed me a photo of himself in disguise. It was audacious in its simplicity. 'I have to pick where I do it. Can't do that everywhere.'

There was a method to it, he explained. 'If the friends in your group give you *bhaav*, then the crowd will know from their behaviour. I tell them, "Just be normal. Do not defer to me. Then people know this must be somebody." Suppose

I have to go to Spencer Plaza, I will blend with the crowd and walk through. And once when I was walking in a mall, three guys behind me commented, "Who does he think he is? Vikram?" My strategy worked!'

Vikram continued, 'I'll go to shops and pick up stuff.' But it depends on the area. 'You can't go into T Nagar or Mylapore. Anyone will get mobbed there, a serial artist or comedian will get mobbed, not just me. Besant Nagar is more cosmopolitan.'

In fact, he is determined not to let stardom affect him. 'Being normal is a beautiful thing. Many actors miss that because of the wall they build around themselves. When you go to hospital, you have to go yourself!'

In this respect, 'I am a little different from other actors who will not go to a normal gym. Rather they will go to a 5-star gym where nobody talks to them, or work out at home. They will not go shopping and some are even remote from their own kids. The moment they walk into the room there's a flurry. *Appa vandaachu*, Father's come! Switch off the television, go to your room.

'In my case, if I am watching a channel my kids will come and say, "We want to watch something else", and I have to change it. Very normal, that way. Even in their school, I tell the other kids, "I am an uncle here, do not come and ask me for autographs, pictures, just ignore me." Then they got used to me.'

Vikram famously protects his family from unwanted publicity and the cameras, so that they can do the things they want to without being pointed at. But 'the bane of actors is mobile cameras. It is not about taking the picture with you, their favourite actor, it is about putting it on their Facebook wall. I am so averse to it. At airports if you stop for a second, you will get caught, which is fine but not when I am with my family.'

And with increasing nation-wide fame, after *Raavan* and *David*, 'In Bombay, people are recognizing me which is nice.' And in a wistful tone he added. 'They don't come and disturb you.'

There is a close relationship between the world of cinema and politics in Tamil Nadu. But, unlike so many other actors who have ridden on the vote-bank of their fans to form political parties and contest elections, Vikram draws the line at entering politics. 'Power does not interest me. I'm not made for it. It is not my passion. I don't think I could do that.'

And so, fourteen years after Sethu, what does it feel like to walk into public places and hear his songs being played, or scenes from his movies on television?

'It has become normal to hear my songs in a room. I don't watch half the interviews given by me. Every Sunday there is a movie of mine playing on television.' Vikram offered an analogy. 'It's like you are growing up and then you go through the ugly duckling stage and then you are beautiful and then after a point you don't look in the mirror.'

The other reason is that, being a perfectionist, 'Every picture of mine that I see, I tell myself – *Shit I could have done that better. Ohhh, I should've held this pose one second less, one second more.* So I don't watch my movies. Also, in Tamil Nadu should they see me in the theatre it would create a disturbance. I sit in the cabin and watch the response. My fans ... the first few scenes they will be screaming and clapping for everything I do onscreen. But later there is a time ... they do not know you are there ... and the general audience – not just your fans – when *they* clap it is a nice feeling.'

But for an actor, the abiding desire is, 'You *want* an audience ... that is always there. Then so much of an audience becomes normal. So how do you increase your audience, take it to a higher level?'

Twenty-four years after his first film, Vikram can reflect with pride, 'I was always focused on this ... that I had to become an actor who's acclaimed, whom people talk about. And I have achieved that. People say I am one of the finest actors in India, people appreciate me and this does not sound modest but...'

It's the truth.

10

The Birth of a Citizen

'Patients ask me, "How long before I can make chapattis again?"'
Dr Uma Ram

Time in Madras has a slow, attenuated quality for there is no pressure of the kind that a belief in a single life to live might create. Counted in terms of kalpa, one day in Brahma the Creator's life equals to 4.32 billion human years. One's idea of time thus expanded to infinity, as it were, the life-span allotted to a human being, rarely exceeding 120 years, seems paltry.

While the city has adopted the Gregorian calendar, at the workplace, in school, to make travel plans or celebrate anniversaries – indeed Seshadri mentioned the growing importance of January 1 – its secret rhythms are attuned to the lunar calendar. The festivals all arrive, as they have for centuries, on the particular lunar day, the *tithi*. The panchangam detailing these is a necessity in most homes. Perhaps the only events linked to the transit of the sun are the harvest festival of Pongal in January, and Tamil New Year's day in April.

The first signs of an approaching festival are to be seen in the marketplace. Makeshift stalls are erected, heaps of flowers quickly threaded into garlands, clay images displayed, urchins pester one to buy puja accessories from them, and thickets of banana fronds and pyramids of fruit appear by the side of the road. Sacks of puffed rice tell you it is time for Ayudha puja, painted clay dolls signal Navaratri and long stalks of sugarcane, purple skin intact, announce Pongal. Even though cattle have been relocated to the outskirts of the city, it is still possible on Mattu Pongal to see cows and bulls taken for a bath in the sea at the Marina, and then paraded with gaily decorated horns and bells around their necks.

In the Tamil month of Margazhi, women wake up early to decorate the threshold with large, elaborate kolams. On a narrow street, the auspicious kolam may spread from one side to the other. Great care is taken not to repeat the designs, great pride taken in tracing the finest of dots and curving lines on the earth with rice flour. Some things may have changed – inflation has meant replacing rice flour with chalk powder; ready-made kolam mats are available; enamel paint can make it permanent – but the creative instinct to beautify one's home, be it a simple hut or enormous bungalow, has not altered. And in this, the city dweller is no different from her cousin in the village.

The day before Vinayaka Chaturthi, jostled by the crowd, distracted by the cries of the vendors, I too search among the many similar images – made of a mould, with red beads for eyes – for the one Ganesha that attracts me the most, who says 'Take me home.'

I remember looking forward as a child to Vinayaka Chaturthi, even more than Deepavali. It was part of a yearly celebration that happened in other homes, not mine where Deepavali was the main event, and it acquired an aura of great mystery.

That was the day I got to eat *kozhukattais* prepared by generous aunties who invariably made some extra for me. I approved entirely of Ganesha's love for the coconut-and-jaggery filled offerings – these miniature sacks of steamed flour collapsed in the mouth yielding the deliciously sweet morsels hidden within them.

All of a sudden, there was a special presence in those homes, a figure whose rotund belly and curved trunk no amount of freshly plucked flowers could hide. Often I would arrive there after the puja was done and the incense-laden smoke hovered over the benign god, making it seem as though an ethereal mist had accompanied him from the heavens. In each home, Ganesha looked different for he took on the shades of light and decoration and atmosphere and piety apparent there. There was a glow on every face, the satisfaction of having honoured a guest in the right way at the right time.

Of all the symbolism associated with this festival, perhaps the most powerfully visual and yet persuasively subtle is the act of immersing the idol. Having accepted our devotion, Ganesha refuses to stay in our homes for long. People trudge through sand, carefully carrying their foot-high idol to the beach. Along the seashore, idols are set down facing east, a brief waving of camphor, and it is time to say goodbye. On returning home, the spot he occupied seems bereft of all cheer.

Madras or Chennai, the special days of celebration punctuate the long unspooling of a year, creating personal memories along the way. A festival engenders a curious relationship with time: there is no way to prolong the festivities. When the nine days of Navaratri are over, they are over; one can neither extend nor shorten the celebration. And that tension, that it will both arrive and inexorably end, is what lends a keen edge to the event.

Deepavali begins pre-dawn, on Naraka Chaturdashi, when a sesame oil bath is a must and new clothes are worn. I have always been struck by the fact that the bombs and firecrackers – that people start lighting with great abandon at 5 a.m. – stop in the skies as though by common consent as soon as the new-moon night of Deepavali is over. Children who have hoarded their crackers do burst their store in the days to come but somehow it lacks the mass energy created when people, rich or poor, come together in celebration.

A death in the family and the subsequent non-participation in festivals for a year pushes one into a separate loop of time. When my father passed away, it felt strange not to be in the flow of Deepavali festivity, to maintain a little pool of darkness when a million lamps were lit in the neighbourhood. At such a time, remembering my father's conviction that each day is a festival, that there is an ongoing daily celebration of life not restricted to festivals alone, helped to fill his absence.

Each year, I look forward to visiting my friend, Dr Uma Ram during Navaratri, to see the display of *golu* dolls at her home. She is a reputed gynaecologist, very popular and busy, but has managed to balance running her home and her clinic, her personal and professional life, with seeming ease.

I reached early, hoping we would get to talk before the other guests arrived.

As was customary, Uma had cleared her living room of most of its furniture to make space for a small cloth-draped flight of steps. Clay gods and goddesses were arranged on the topmost tier. Ranged below were mythological characters and famous temples. To look at them was to also recognize traditional groupings, the eight Lakshmis, the six famous shrines of Muruga, the ten avatars of Vishnu, Ganesha beneath a peepul tree, and a baby Krishna.

They were a reminder that myths are integrated into our daily lives. These stories set in other worlds, other eras, are ever-present, ever-relevant in the Indian universe, for our festivals serve as links across the centuries. This is most true of Navaratri, when women celebrate both the power of Shakti and their own femininity.

Soon we were seated cross-legged on the floor, picking figures out of a cardboard box … animals, cricketers, a bangle-seller … as Uma gave me insights into her world.

'On Monday mornings between 7.30 and 9 a.m., I can be reasonably certain I will not be starting surgery.' That is the dreaded one-and-a-half hours of the day when the mythical being Rahu, one half of a snake, is said to rule. Nothing auspicious is to be undertaken at this time, for he will ruin its outcome. No social visits, no marriage ceremony, no house-warming, no purchase of a new car, and certainly, perish the thought, no pre-planned entry into this world for it would mean problems with the birth and throughout life.

Talking to her, it became fascinatingly obvious that this juncture between pregnancy and childbirth, when the city welcomes a newborn citizen, is its secret core where scientists delink from rational thinking in their own lives and age-old customs are followed blindly while new technology is both assimilated and misused.

'I am faced constantly with the question of time. If I post a C-section for Monday morning, the patients will refuse. The fear of *Rahu kaalam* permeates *all* communities. One might assume that for a non-Hindu, Rahu kaalam will not matter but it does. They say "you know what is a good time, doctor," indirectly telling me to avoid Rahu kaalam!

'The classic juxtaposition of tradition versus modernity truly comes up when a child is being born. There are people who give me seven to ten minute windows for the delivery. They may have consulted me for nine months, but if I do not agree to a caesarean at that given delivery time, a few will go away and have a C-section elsewhere.'

A person's life unravels to the map of the heavens, set at the time of birth. Given the deeply rooted belief in Vedic astrology, when it comes to elective surgery families hope to ensure a 'good' time of birth – when the planets form propitious conjunctions – and voila, a good life will follow. If only it were that simple! Ravana tried to do it aeons ago, marshalling all the planets into one house of the zodiac when his son Meghnad was born, but wily Saturn foiled his plan. Clearly we haven't learnt from Ravana's example.

The attempt to manipulate fate, continued Uma, 'also relates to specific stars or *nakshatrams*.' For example, there is the belief that if someone is born in Rohini, Krishna's *nakshatra*, the child's uncle will suffer. 'When a patient suggested avoiding that period, I retorted, "If you have an uncle such as Kamsa … maybe it's not so bad after all." They were so annoyed with me!'

As Uma burst into laughter, I registered anew her genuine sense of caring and warm, wide smile. Dressed in a blue silk sari with a mauve border, there was nothing of the forbidding-doctor-in-a-white-coat about her.

'So the mother-to-be will make a request based on the stars, "Today is a good day, induce me. Either the baby should be born today or two days later." It is just impossible! I know as a doctor that if I begin a process of induction, it is a bit of a sham, for no one will deliver within six hours. I try and explain to them but it seems simpler to say, "Okay. Do a caesarean. Have the baby when you want."'

This takes the idea of elective surgery, or the caesarean, into a grey area. 'A patient said she would pay me double if I did an elective C-section at midnight! Another time, a professor at the Indian Institute of Technology phoned me. His daughter was due in May, but he wanted her to deliver in April. I said, "That is way too early, an entire month. Why?" He replied,

"It will be the month of Chitrai," as per the Tamil calendar, "should not have a child then." When it comes to private personal decisions, even men of science lose that rationality.'

It results in Uma constantly having to weigh her medical decisions. 'I was torn, should I stick to my conscience and say 'No', or do it for the sake of the girl who is my patient.'

But the worst is in homes where the marriage was arranged and the girl, new entrant, dependent, is viewed with suspicion. 'Once, when it became clear I had to induce a patient, two or three relatives came to enquire if I was going to do it on a particular day, which was not auspicious. I said, "No." Later the girl said, "My in-laws do not trust me and they thought I had deliberately fixed that day with you. When I remonstrated, my husband hit me." ' Exclaimed Uma, 'Physical abuse of a pregnant woman! And she was full term. The husband tried to justify his behavior, blaming her. I told him it was a punishable offence!'

Physically abused, because she might have taken the liberty of fixing the date her child was to be born without consulting her in-laws.

'The amount of physical abuse bothers me. Educated women too, not just the poor or uneducated.' When a young woman feels she has no support in her in-laws home or no elder to reach out to in a nuclear family, 'by default when she visits a doctor, it spills out. The physical abuse of women is far more than we imagine it to be. One girl said they tied her legs to the bedpost to ensure that she did not walk for two or three days once her pregnancy was confirmed. I was appalled. It was a well-to-do family.'

We had a complete set of cricketers. Now we needed a field. While Uma was busy shaking a fine layer of green rangoli powder onto the floor, I had time to muse. Her home is very close to the clinic run by her, EV Kalyani Medical Centre, which had a personal significance for me: I was born there.

EV Kalyani was married and widowed while still a child, in the twenties, which meant that little Kalyani would have to live the rest of her life deprived of many of its joys, her head shaved, wearing plain cloth, no blouse, and shorn of all adornment. Her father EV Srinivasan was resolute in his aim of giving his daughter her life back. His decision to put her through medical school, specializing in obstetrics, resulted in his being ostracized from his own family. Undeterred, he moved out of the family home, to Egmore, and lived there until she finished her studies, becoming the first woman MD in Tamil Nadu. They then returned to Mylapore where he built the nursing home for her to work in, the first of its kind in India. Presiding over the birth of scores of babies, legendary Dr Kalyani helped many women get access to medical care at a time when deliveries usually took place at home.

In the remarkable way that lives are interconnected, Uma, my childhood friend from school, became a doctor, married Dr Kalyani's nephew Dr Ram Rajagopal and worked at EVK with Dr Gita Arjun after finishing her post-graduate degree. We had our sons a week apart in the same place and recently, she had taken on the almost sacred task of preserving Dr Kalyani's legacy.

In a city where some of the country's most famous doctors were also Brahmin, Uma's own family's history illustrates how caste rules and modern medicine were accommodated decades ago.

Uma continued, 'My aunt Bama Rajagopal was the first girl in the family to study medicine. Her grandfather, my paternal great-grandfather Dr Seethapathy Iyer, once brought a diarrhoea patient home, which could have been potentially cholera, and his daughters stood there holding the drip till it finished since there was no stand. Bama grew up in this atmosphere and getting into science, medicine was natural to her.

'At the same time, because they were doing dissections on human cadavers, when she returned from college, she would have to go to the back of the house, have a bath and only then enter the house. This was literally following the rules of pollution for a death. By the time it came to me, after a dissection in college, we went through the day and came home, normally. And now, my son's friends tell me they dissect on cadavers without gloves, which is so unhygienic! But that's the sort of change in the past seventy-five years.'

Dr Seethapathy Iyer, the first Indian to head King's Institute 'got his daughters married late, by the standards of those times, after college.' Passionate about music, he wanted his daughters to be taught by the best. Who else but the great Dhanammal, the incomparable musician? However, the conventions of those times meant that 'it was not done for a Brahmin to take his daughter to Dhanammal's home to learn', given her devadasi background. Dr Seethapathy simply arranged for Dhanammal to visit his home, where she then taught his daughters. When he employed non-Brahmin servants, part of the help he gave to a lot of families in his neighbourhood, it meant that the Kanchi Paramacharya would not enter his house and the good doctor had to honour him outside on the road.

'Certain families were very progressive, probably far more progressive than we are today. Daughters were given an education, allowed to take up sport, learn music.' And it is fitting in a way, that the children of Dr Seethapathy's daughters kept the family interest in medicine alive by becoming doctors. In 1963, Uma's father, NS Murali, a legendary doctor himself, and aunt, Dr Sarojini, started a clinic named after their grandfather.

In 2000, Uma moved from EV Kalyani Medical Centre to practice at Seethapathy Clinic. The years of working with and learning from her father were extremely special. After her father passed away, Uma and her brother Dr Sandeep, a surgeon, jointly run Seethapathy Clinic. Dr Sarojini still has her practice there and with amazing energy continues to see patients even on Sunday. In 2013, life came full circle as it were and Uma extended her practice to EV Kalyani Medical Centre. As this is close to both her home and the Seethapathy Clinic, she is able to run both clinics with an able and like-minded group that she has carefully built over the years.

Setting wickets and a hunched-over umpire at the centre of a green oval, Uma talked about how she often finds the things she takes for granted, born of her own liberal upbringing coupled with a conservative convent-school education, at odds with what is the dismal everyday reality of some of her female patients.

'There was a patient who would come at the end of the day, without an appointment, or in the middle of the afternoon, and insist on being seen. When I told her, "You can't walk in like this. You have to respect my time as well," she broke down, sobbing, "I can leave the house only if my father-in-law allows me." There are lots of families like this,' exclaimed Uma.

She is equally flummoxed by the preference for baby boys, and the contradiction in terms when fathers and mothers-to-be frankly articulate this to Uma, their very accomplished, highly educated and all too *feminine* doctor. 'There is a lot of value placed on having a boy baby, especially in some communities. It is not uncommon – them wanting sex determination for a termination. I don't do it. But as long as there are doctors willing, it will not end. There are people who sympathize with the women and actively help terminate it.'

And this desire can be traced to the rules governing Hindu death ceremonies, for the birth of a son assures the father that on a future day his soul will find release when his son lights his funeral pyre. 'It is there in our psyche. Take the terrible things described in the *Garuda Puranam*, like a sort of hell … it is possible to cross all of them *if* you have a son who does your death rites.'

Uma had a faraway look in her eyes as she spoke, 'One of the earliest things I remember, when I had just graduated from Madras Medical College,' one of the top medical colleges in the country, 'and started working at EVK. There were two very old nurses from Dr EV Kalyani's times. When it happened that a woman in labour was not pushing actively, these nurses would comment, "She is scared that it will be another girl." At that time, being young, I could not believe it but now I think there maybe some truth in it.'

For Uma has seen the sort of dismay with which the birth of a girl is received. 'The reaction is immediate, as soon as you deliver and show the baby to the mother. Her face will crumple, "Tcha, *phir ladki hui*. Another girl." It is as though she has failed. How terrible for a woman to feel like that, and the fact that society makes you feel that way is terrible. I often tell them, "Look around you in this room, is there anyone male here? Why do you feel bad about having a girl?"'

Worse, 'some will refuse to feed the newborn, or keep crying, so we have to be vigilant. It means for the mother that inevitably she will have to attempt one more pregnancy, so even these women's mothers feel bad.'

Having said that, Uma finds there are a great many people who welcome and cherish a girl. Interestingly, parents adopting a child usually choose a girl and there are the rare exceptions who are disappointed at the birth of a boy.

'There!' The last fielder was at square leg and a cricket match was in full swing within the green oval.

Part of the delight of golu is the trouble taken to recreate various locales in miniature. Uma had a bed of earth ready with sprouted grain. The tiny leaves and slender stalks were perfect for a jungle. Stones became rocks, and crunched up blue glasspaper a stream for fish. Here a tiger, there a deer … I handed her the animals one by one.

Given that Uma lives in a nuclear family, free of some of the more onerous demands of a joint family situation, she has to carefully evaluate some of the seemingly innocuous questions posed to her. Such as the one asked by a Marwari woman who had just delivered – *How long before I can make chapattis again?*

'The chapatti one was classic,' chuckled Uma. 'Thinking of my own home where we make maybe seven or eight, maximum, I said, "It's fine, you can start as soon as you return home." But this girl needed to make thirty to thirty-five chapattis for just one meal! So for her to knead the dough, stand on her feet and make all of them in a hot kitchen was a bigger task than I imagined!

'I'm constantly learning to assess questions, to see which answer would help my patient. *"Can I travel?"* Customarily, a girl returns to her maternal home for the first few weeks after childbirth but if the travelling involves four days of a bus journey immediately after delivery, and the girl does not want to undertake it, I have to figure it out from her body language. Equally if a girl is desperate to go back to her mother's home, but her in-laws refuse to send her, I will have to balance things out and say that she needs the rest, that they should send her.'

The characteristics of different communities also play a part in the care for the pregnant woman. 'It is very interesting to be a gynaecologist, I learn so much about our social structures. I think the Marwaris are perhaps the only community which displays the strength of a joint family. They offer a lot of support … the aunts and sisters-in-law will come and support each other. They are a bit hesitant about allowing the husbands to come in to the delivery room.'

Once married, the pressure on a woman to have a child is enormous. To be barren is perhaps the worst misfortune. Yet, in a day, Uma's patients might range from a woman who, despite learning that the cleft palate in her foetus could be surgically healed on birth, had an abortion because she feared being shamed in the village, to one desperate to have a baby. 'A professor broke down when she had her second miscarriage. She wailed, "You will not understand. I come from a very small village, the interior of southern Tamil Nadu where children do not finish school. My father sent me to school, college all the way up to my MPhil. I may be teaching in the city but when I go back to the village, I am *not* a mother *yet*. That is a disgrace, like a black mark, I have not achieved what is important." I felt so sad to hear her say that.'

Ironically, with more women working, 'couples often don't have the time to meet, leave alone mate.

'There are a lot of couples both working different shifts who come to me for infertility. And I have to literally explain the biology involved in making a baby! Those who work in the IT or banks, the highly educated group who are too cerebral, they mess it up often! One husband said to me, "I am used to putting in the effort and getting the reward. I topped my studies, did an MBA, got a job and am successful. *Why* am I not able to have a baby?" The cause was unexplained infertility, a big crisis for him.'

And then, 'There are quite a few men who have no idea what to do, who have not consummated the marriage for six or seven years. The man does not realize that full penetration has not happened.' Here, at least, a happy outcome is quite possible, post-counselling.

At the other extreme, there are people who take budding life so casually as to want to end it for the most whimsical of reasons. 'One couple requested termination because there was going to be a *griha-pravesham*, house-warming, and she would not be able to 'sit' or participate in the ceremony. I refused to do it. Another woman wanted termination because she did not want to miss a project in Australia. In India, we have very liberal termination laws, but people want to abort for the flimsiest of reasons!'

Uma paused to reflect on a tough scenario she dealt with. 'There was a lady, seven or eight weeks pregnant, who came to me requesting an MTP. Legally, it is enough if the woman signs the consent form. She got admitted, and was inside the theatre, on the table, just about to be anaes-thetized when her husband arrived. He was furious!' When the lady learnt that her husband was waiting outside, she sat bolt upright on the table and cancelled the termination. 'She was petrified of him! It was the third pregnancy and she did not want it, but the friend who was supposed to help her, chickened out and informed the husband. What is right, what is wrong? There is the law, the rules on one hand and then dealing with human beings, feelings, makes it very complicated.'

Such a situation could have been prevented by the use of contraceptives but that is another fraught area.

To begin with, what ought to be the most private compact between a husband and wife is conducted with the involvement of others. 'Some mothers-in-law keep track of sexual activity … when it occurred the last time, or allowing the couple to be together only when she decides. It still happens, and there are men who agree to all this without protesting.

'Many a time a father-in-law will come into the consulting room with his son and daughter-in-law. Even as I tell him politely to leave, he will say, "I do not know if they are doing it properly." In front of her!

'Let's say after all of this, a girl does have two children and wants to stop. In the majority of middle-class families, she will have to ask her husband, *and* get the permission of the mother-in-law. Sometimes when the husband is supportive they will take the pill and ask that the mother-in-law not be told. It is tricky keeping track of all of this!'

Commented Uma, 'There are a lot of things which we do not even imagine because in our milieu we are so used to seeing women empowered that we forget many women can't make a choice. Even with something as crucial as diet, I've learnt there are women who don't control what is cooked in their house. So there is no point in telling her about the optimal diet, we have to tackle the person who actually decides the meal. It is all about control and lack of choice.'

Having interacted with hundreds of families, Uma has this to say, 'Very rarely are individual decisions made by the couple. Reproductive choice is always decided *with* the family, so I end up counselling all of them. And the key decision-maker is not always a parent, it could be a spinster aunt who wields authority. Also, unlike in the West, confidentiality is not a given. I can't promise my patient, the girl, that I won't tell. That would put her in greater trouble.'

The unforgettable anecdote Uma shared with me revealed so much about the changing city and unchanging attitudes.

In a culture where pre-marital chastity is paramount, a sixteen-year-old schoolgirl became pregnant. She came to Uma's clinic accompanied by her mother, father, grandparents, the boy, the boy's parents and soon it was very crowded inside the consultation room. It seemed to me that their presence would have both comforted and daunted the young girl. Later, having terminated the pregnancy, when Uma wanted to talk to the girl about contraception, her father got very annoyed saying that such knowledge would only get his daughter into worse trouble!

Uma sighed. 'Increase in pre-marital sex is a fact of life. This generation of children is very blasé about relationships. The sanctity is no longer there ... that it is special, that it is a significant moment.' Earlier, to even ask the question "Are you sexually active?" would have been insulting. Now Uma goes a step further and asks, albeit gently – 'that's the irony, *I* hesitate – "Same partner?" And they say "No." They are not sensible either, they don't use contraceptives, which is scary with all the prevalent STDs.'

The box was empty; the golu almost done. Uma's jungle was well-populated with wildlife. At the very bottom of her stepped display, she began to recreate market scenes, a pot-bellied Chettiar tradesman and his wife selling sacks of pulses, potters, weavers ... The bangle-seller took his place at the end.

'From being a women's affair, more husbands are present at delivery – that has increased, across communities. It is a result of being doctor-encouraged and greater social awareness.' Uma paused to reflect upon our own prejudices, 'Some men you little expect it of – tradition-bound, ordinary looking men, are hugely supportive of their wives while some of the smartly dressed, with-it ones can be total morons.'

Perhaps the most drastic change has been in the number of children a couple has. 'While in our parents' generation, eight to thirteen children were common, the average now is two. Even here, community-based patterns are clear. Marwaris will definitely have two children. If both turn out to be girls, they will attempt a third. Families that are involved in commerce, Muslims, or the well-to-do will all have more children, whereas a middle-class Hindu is very unlikely to have a second.'

Interestingly, adoption of technology has overridden a key belief, that of shielding a newborn from the evil eye, until it has a chance to thrive. 'Even before it is wiped, wrapped and brought out, they want to post it on FB and Twitter. The idea of shielding it from *kannu*, the malefic evil eye, is completely gone. The photo is taken in a jiffy!'

Uma returned to the topic of auspicious days that we had begun with. While the desire that it should be at a 'good' time still influences the birth of a child, and people will cancel a scan fixed for Rahu kaalam, in other ways the old mores are changing.

'Earlier, say ten years ago, even if the clinic were open on the festival days of Pongal no one would come. Or take Varalakshmi vratham, the festival where women worship the goddess for a long, happy marital life, hardly anyone would show up. The norm was that you would not leave home, forget combining a trip to the hospital with the festivities.'

Today patients, especially the more westernized ones, suit their own convenience. 'Those who work, especially in the IT sector, find a holiday convenient to visit the doctor. So the link between auspicious day and we-will-not-go-anywhere, that link is erased.'

Dr Uma drew on the experience of generations of doctors in her family to assess changes within the medical community itself. 'At the time I think there were few but good medical colleges. There were some very influential and successful doctors who served society at large. Chiefly, they were idealistic. Medicine at that time was seen as a vocation. You *served* people. Today that service concept has gone. It has become more commercial, more corporatized, impersonal and people's attitudes have changed equally.'

Part of being a gynaecologist is accepting the fact that the hours are long. 'There is a heavy work load, you are just one person, you cannot be available 24/7, so you try and finish work more efficiently.' But in the next generation, 'I now come across medicos who finish their qualifying exams in gynae but don't want to do the long hours, won't do nights, schedule deliveries between 9 a.m. to 6 p.m. and shift to a sub-speciality which gives them control over their work timing. The whole purpose of being a gynaecologist is defeated!'

Paradoxically, 'Since there are more options to induce labour, done safely when it is a medical reason, it is being extended for social reasons. It is really a grey area.'

There was one last thing left to do. Uma placed a foot-high idol of Durga, victorious in killing Mahishasura, on the middle of the steps. 'This is what I bought this year,' she said and we admired the image for a while. The waves of hair around the smiling face, the tireless arms clutching many weapons and the energy in her posture. 'Done!' exclaimed Uma.

A doctor is quite close to god in this city, held in great degrees of awe and veneration. Usually, there is implicit trust. And that is what pains Uma, the sense that wrong ethics and the wrong sort of commercialization – where a junior doctor is under pressure to earn back the crores paid to study medicine – results in a violation of that trust. 'You don't really care about what is in the best interests of the patient … when money and commerce become a bigger part of the equation. We need to break this attitude, for medicine to be delivered in the way it should be.'

Uma went on to talk about perhaps the most trying day of her career, 'The absolute worst is to have a mother die. Once, a woman came in complaining of intense back pain. She was in an advanced state of pregnancy, her heart beat was slowing down. As soon as I opened her up, I realized we were in trouble, because she was bleeding somewhere else which I could not control. I delivered the baby and got additional cardiac help but it was too late. She had an aorta that dissected, an extremely rare complication.'

While trying her best to save the patient's life, Uma had also the difficult task of keeping the family informed. 'They were very calm. "Okay, you just go back and try resuscitating her and we will pray." There was no anger, no questioning which made me feel even worse, not that I could have prevented her death.' Two weeks later, the bereaved husband returned, to reassure Uma, saying they knew she had done her best.

'I wanted to cry that day. What it would have taken him to come and say that! The trust people put in you ... makes you wonder if you are worthy of that. So you *give* what makes you worthy of that trust. That's why it bothers me when I see a casual prescription made by another doctor, because people come to you with trust and you *cannot* break that.'

Needless to say, all of this must have an emotional toll on the human being Uma who happens to be a doctor. 'One gets quite involved in some of these situations. It saps you at the end of the day, if you have two three of the complicated ones.'

A place where babies are born has happy energies. What does it feel like to preside over that space where a young woman delivers a baby, and a mother is born?

'The thrill of a baby being born … it is a phenomenal rush. Every time, every single time, it is an amazing feeling. I am amazed at physiology and the body's ability to make something like this happen, for life to create life. Earlier today, we had twins, a boy and a girl and it was so lovely to be able to say to the parents, "Here! These are yours to keep." However tired you are, no matter the time of night or day, that pleasure is guaranteed.'

Guests began to arrive; female; of all ages. Women floated in and out, wearing beautiful silks and jewellery, tailed by their daughters patently thrilled to be all dressed up in long skirts or *pavadai*. Some could be persuaded to sing, in praise of the goddesses Durga, Lakshmi and Saraswati, while others were shy. We sat on the floor listening to impromptu concerts, surrounded by the heady fragrance of flowering jasmines.

I managed to escape before some bright soul asked me to sing, but not before Uma had given me a basket filled with a set of coasters, an earthern lamp, turmeric-kumkum and betel leaves-*supari*. She may have substituted these for the comb-mirror-blouse piece of her mother's times but one thing had remained unchanged. I eagerly pulled out a packet of *sundal*, demolishing the chickpeas flavoured with green chillies and coconut shavings as I walked down her driveway.

On to another home I had been invited to, another array of dolls and lots more sundal. Only here, the chickpeas had been replaced, in an attempt at innovation, by sweetcorn kernels. Whatever next!

11

Building Peace

'In my childhood, the windows of homes were all left open.'
A Faizur Rahman

One abiding feature of Madras was the 'garden house', built by the wealthy, whether European, British or Indian. Beginning with the late seventeenth century, sprawling bungalows with thick walls and high ceilings were set in the midst of a large tract of land, part lawn, part orchard. A lime coating – *chunam* made of seashells, egg whites and sugar, of which the precise ratio has been lost – ensured that the walls dazzled white.

Today, it is difficult to find these 'garden houses' as they have either been demolished or are being used for other purposes such as schools. However, deep in the heart of one of the last surviving green parcels of land, is situated Mowbray's Cupola, once owned by perhaps the richest man in Madras, the Portuguese merchant John D'Monte. Apart from the unusual cupola, some of the other standard features are visible – a high portico, stout round pillars, breezy verandahs, a flat roof and numerous rooms including an octagonal hall and large ballroom, though the building itself, now home to the exclusive Madras Club, is not accessible to all.

John D'Monte died heirless and willed his substantial holdings of property across the city to the Church. Income derived from this estate was to be used for the welfare of widows, orphans, and other charitable avenues. It is thanks to his generosity of spirit that many of the 109 acres, part of Mowbray's Gardens surrounding his house, have escaped being built over or 'developed'. The houses in one part, D'Monte Colony, now abandoned, are said to be haunted by ghosts. In the way that connections are drawn at random, the vast premises of the college I studied in, Stella Maris, occupy what was once known as The Cloisters, also owned by D'Monte.

The wealthy apart, the juxtaposition of the two words, garden and house, applied to the smallest of houses in the city, even of brick and thatch. Anyone who had any land at all put it to good use, growing all sorts of edible greens and plants. Sometimes, a sapling planted on the side of a public road was watched over and guarded, and later its fruits shared.

All sorts of people, known and unknown, take a proprietorial interest in one's garden. I used to wonder why so many neighbours wanted to visit my garden until I discovered a betel leaf creeper nestled in an innocuous corner. There was a cluster of banana trees that never produced fruit thus making them perfect for other purposes. Trustees of a local temple celebrating a festival asked me if they could cart away several of those to make decorations from. Just how they knew about those barren trees I will never know.

One neighbour felt that she had permanent visiting rights and usually made her raids before dawn. Having watched a rose-bud swell in size, I woke early one morning dying to see the first blossom on the plant only to find a headless stalk; she had beaten me to it. If ever the desire for murder most foul rose in my heart, it was then! And who has not been approached at least once by neighbours wanting mango leaves or neem or drumstick or curry leaves? Is there any point in saying 'No'?

Many still believe, as I do, in the idea that a home and its garden are inseparable. But clearly we are outnumbered.

I'm filled with dismay whenever I see houses all over Chennai being pulled down, gardens decimated, and concrete sealing every square inch of the land. The story is the same everywhere: Elderly parents find it difficult to manage spacious garden-homes without servants, and wishing to ensure an amicable division of their property between children, they convert their homes into several self-contained apartments. The neem tree opposite my house, whose spreading branches were axed to make space for one such apartment complex to flourish, has never regained its splendour.

As real estate prices vault, the city is shorn of greenery and the sense of leisure that a garden affords. What it tells us about ourselves is disturbing. To my mind it reveals a shrinking inwards – a voluntary relinquishing of an invaluable dimension of life and an unconscious yielding to gross materiality. A wealth commonly available to anyone owning land in the city, the delight of watching plants grow, is paradoxically becoming something only the rich possess.

To understand some of the enormous changes in the city related to land and attitudes to it, I sought out Faizur Rahman, a civil engineer who runs a construction business.

We journeyed to Old Washermanpet, an area far north of the city, predominantly Muslim, to revisit his childhood days. Faizur Rahman, 'call me Faiz, same as the poet,' had not been here in a year, and I, never.

By the early eighteenth century, the cotton trade begun from Fort St. George was such a commercial success that more space was needed for the many artisans connected with the supply of cotton, its weaving, bleaching, dyeing, painting; all of the expanding industry that anchored and enriched the East India Company's presence in the city. As its name suggests, fabric from the looms was sent to the dhobis or 'washermen' settled in this new area, north of the Fort, to be washed and treated.

Nearly 300 years on, Faiz did not recall seeing many dhobis in his childhood. 'Maybe now they are limited to a much smaller area.'

The street was narrow, maybe ten feet across. Houses rose right off the street, walls painted in bright colours, pinks, yellows, green, though the home Faiz grew up in was a cool white with blue edges. The buildings loomed on either side, and at some points there was an overhang where they almost touched. I dropped my head far back, to look up at the roofs. Unlike the areas I was used to, there were no gardens, no walls surrounding the properties.

Along the street, the windows set in these fortress walls were closed against the heat and the perennial dust. 'In my childhood, they were all left open,' commented Faiz.

We stood outside a brown wooden door set low in the wall, his maternal grandmother's house, and Faiz pointed diagonally across to a much larger two-storeyed building a hop, skip and a jump away; his father's home.

'I was born to very traditional parents. My father Hakim Mohammad Anwar was from Vaniyambadi and mother Rahmathunnisa from Chennai. Father settled here after education and marriage. My paternal grandmother was so traditional, she insisted that my mother must not walk to her mother's house,' said Faiz, gesturing towards the white house.

'So whenever she came home to see her mother or returned to her marital home, there was a lot of drama. I would be dispatched to get a cycle rickshaw. When the man asked me where the destination was, I would say "Just come", careful never to answer that question. Then he would park outside this door, a screen would be raised and my mother would seat herself in purdah. Barely would he start pedalling, and the door of my father's house appeared, we would yell "Stop!"'

Faiz laughed as he described the hilarious scenario. In a city known for long prolonged negotiations between driver and driven about the distance and the fare, whether cycle or auto rickshaw, just to imagine Faiz's plight was to chuckle.

'My mother was one of the most selfless people I knew,' continued Faiz. 'My father's relatives from the smaller towns would visit our home, not one or two but many at a time, and she would be stuck in the kitchen from morning to night cooking for all of them. *We*, her children, found it an inconvenience ... our studies were disturbed, we could not enquire when they were leaving ... but she never complained. She was generous in spirit, serving them, tending to the sick. I don't think I could be like her at all!'

To the left of his grandmother's home, and opposite his father's house, lay a mosque. 'I grew up in the shadow of a mosque,' said Faiz, 'literally.'

Freshly painted and clean, it is one of the few mosques in the city to allow women to offer namaz on Fridays.

'In those days the mosque was very moderate. The thought of extremism never entered our mind. It was a very inclusive place, never a communal feeling.

'When not in school, we were in the mosque usually. Lots of interactions with the scholars, I was taught to read Arabic. The greatness of Arabic is that you can read it as a child, without understanding it ... because of the diacritical marks, anyone can read. You just need to know the alphabet and how it is pronounced. One of the musts for a Muslim boy or girl was memorizing chapters of the Quran. I can still reproduce them!'

Indeed during the course of the conversation, Faiz quoted verses from the Quran to prove many of his points. The sound of Arabic had a musicality all its own.

It was an annual event near the mosque that was to ignite Faiz's study of the Quran. 'I was initiated into thinking independently about Islam by my father. During Ramzan, there were people who made a big show of distributing clothes to the poor. For just one piece of cloth, thick *gaada* cloth, not even fine fabric, people would stream in and wait overnight. One lungi or one sari. To get these two things, both men and women, the streets would be choked. This ten-foot street would be a sea of humanity. Bamboo barricades would be placed to stop more from entering, and when there were no more clothes, they were shouted at and sent back.

'My father was very upset. He was a clean shaven scholar of Islam. He knew Urdu and Persian and wrote poetry. I remember when I was about ten years old, say in 1975, he talked to me questioning the practice. "Yearly once if you distribute clothes will poverty be reduced?" Then he quoted from Chapter 2 of the Quran. '*Laa tubtilu sadaqaatikum bil manni wal aza* which translates as: Do not render your good deeds worthless by hurting beneficiaries or with constant reminders. My father said, "They were pushing and shouting at the same people to whom they were giving those two pieces of cloth, and in the end they did not have enough for all of them so they gave them a few rupees. What have they achieved?" Later on they stopped, though not because of what my father said.

'I did not understand the verse. I asked him, "Is it there in the Quran? Can you show me?" I was very inquisitive. He took the Quran and brought out an English translation for me. He triggered that thirst to know what was there in the Quran. Such a wonderful thing! It changed my life completely.

I had a father like that … who thought it fit to discuss with a ten-year-old boy.' Clearly moved, he paused, and went on to say, 'I wish every Muslim boy learns Arabic to understand the Quran, then the roots of extremism are cut.'

Faiz pushed open the door to his late grandmother's house, where his uncle now lives. 'His wife is bedridden and he has looked after her for the past eight years,' he informed me. We stepped into a narrow passage, its clean ivory walls matching the colour outdoors. It held what sunlight entered in slabs that moved with the hours, so some of the clothes hung there had dried faster than the rest.

His aged uncle appeared, welcoming us into the courtyard, where two small rooms under an old tiled roof were visible, and further inside to meet his wife. 'I was born in this room!' exclaimed Faiz. I peeped into the room, smiling at the elderly lady who sat cross-legged on an enormous bed, peeling potatoes. Freshly dressed in a cotton sari, from her appearance one would not know that she was ailing.

There was a delicious aroma of onion and garlic being fried for a gravy. We sat in a verandah open to a tiny courtyard, where the sounds of the street did not penetrate. The fan whirred slowly above. There was a sense of peace, a feeling that one could be in any part of the previous century, for the outer world was completely blocked from sight. 'Eight of us lived here at one time!' said Faiz's uncle Ishaq Sharief.

The cook brought out some raw meat in a container. I noticed then the age-old implement *aruvamanai*, a slicing blade set in a wooden base, in the courtyard. Squatting, she deftly ran the meat down the sharp curved edge. It might have been vegetables; her gestures were both familiar and timeless.

Faiz continued talking about his father. 'He was not very well-off. He worked in a bank. Still, he would take me by taxi to preparatory school on Broadway, and pick me up in the afternoon. When the timings were changed, he arranged for a cycle rickshaw to take me. Taking Cemetery Road, we had to cross a manned railway crossing. If the rickshaw puller was late even by minutes, the gates would be closed and we would be stuck for at least forty minutes, and I'd miss my school.

'On the way back, if the goods train were passing, it meant reaching home hungry and hours late, even though school ended at 3.30. I remember that vividly, watching the train pass by. A *long* train, never ending!

'I studied in Don Bosco and even went to the church inside the school! We never knew the difference between Hindu or Muslim or Christian. And like all non-Catholics, I studied moral science.'

When he was about ten or eleven, Faiz shifted to another school, on the other side of Washermanpet. 'Apart from the Quran, Father made me read two books by Dale Carnegie, *How to Win Friends and Influence People* and *How to Stop Worrying and Start Living*. By the time I went to college, I had done a regular study of the Quran,' including several translations and many commentaries.

His uncle, who had disappeared for a while, returned bearing two glasses of cold, creamy almond-flavoured milk. The unexpected guest must be made welcome: it was Indian hospitality made visible. 'I am troubling you a lot,' I protested. 'No trouble at all,' he replied, though he had walked in the hot sun to the nearby market for it. In his chequered lungi and white shirt, kind features etched with a thin grey beard, his identity was distinct. Faiz, boyish, clean shaven, in jeans and shirt, was more cosmopolitan.

Almost reading my mind, Faiz confided, 'People often tell me "You don't have a beard, you don't look like a Muslim at all." I tell them I have to *be* a Muslim. It doesn't matter if

I don't look like one to some people. A Muslim is one who stands for peace. Indeed if one were to go by the spirit of Islam, *anyone* who stands for peace is a Muslim. Any other way of life which is devoid of peace, which violates peace is not acceptable to God. In fact, the word Islam means peace. That is the definition but we have understood in such a way that if you miss praying five times a day or do not keep a beard you are not a Muslim. How good or how much of a Muslim you are is going to be decided not on this earth, but on a particular day of judgement by God. Leave that to God to decide. Let *Him* pass judgement.'

We left soon, in order to walk around the neighbourhood. It was noon, and a golden heat lay upon my face and arms, but given the November nip in the air, it was not unpleasant.

Passing the mosque, Faiz said, 'It was a very liberal mosque. The Hindus of the area had great belief in it too. After the evening prayer, they would bring a sick child and ask the imam to recite a prayer and blow on the child.'

Turning left, we approached the main marketplace.

'My father found work in Saudi Arabia. And thanks to that, all of us, four brothers and one sister, were educated. From the age of six, I knew I wanted to build homes, shelters that kept people safe. So I went to Bellary to study Civil Engineering.'

In that small town in Karnataka, Faiz found time to enlarge the scope of his studies. He discovered an affinity for the Thirukkural. 'Valluvar says *Idukkan varungaal naguga* … If you encounter any difficulty, laugh it off. That is the only way out. And in the Quran, Surah 94, *inna ma'al usri yusra* … Indeed, with hardship comes ease. So we should not get disheartened if we encounter difficulties.'

Curious about other religions as well, he read as much as he could. 'One of my good friends was the Bishop of Bellary. We used to discuss religion, and the nice thing about him was that he was open to different views on Christianity and gave me a patient hearing.'

It was in Bellary that an Ahl al-Hadith mosque invited him to speak once a week. 'After the four o' clock prayer, there was a discussion on Islam. It was the biggest achievement of my life, apart from the degree.' It was a very unusual gesture, because Faiz, apart from being very young, had not attended a madrasa and was not a certified scholar, in that sense, of Islam.

When Faiz graduated and was to leave Bellary, 'They were so good ... those people, first time in their history they gave a student this privilege. They held a farewell meeting inside the mosque and honoured me with a shawl. It was very touching, they actually praised me and sent me on my way. I don't think they have done it for anyone. I was the only exception.'

It gave Faiz the confidence to voice his views, his interpretations, seeking a more inclusive approach among his brethren. 'Scholars may disagree with my interpretations, but they know I am serious.'

He has lent his time and scholarship to a unique series of textbooks by Oxford University Press called *Living* in *Harmony* that introduces children to the values and beliefs of all the many religions that exist in India.

Faiz believes with a passion that children ought to be taught to think for themselves. 'They are being given a very narrow-minded view, a coloured vision of the world, creating hatred for the other which is not the Quran. They will not be able to adjust in a multi-religious, multi-cultural multi-ethnic society like India if they are programmed like robots.'

His views are controversial and not accepted by everybody. 'We need more liberal scholars who would rather talk about socio-economic conditions than abstract theology during the sermons at the mosques. Muslims are suffering because their education and economic situation has worsened. In education, we are worse than Dalits according to the Sachar committee report.' To Faiz's dismay, 'Today, one of the custodians of the same mosque in Bellary does not agree with me. So I told him, "Today you may censure me, but don't forget the honour I once received in your mosque."'

On returning to Madras, Faiz trained himself by working on several projects with a building contractor, Hanif Ahmed, who was doing projects for a company called Alsa. 'Alsa was a fantastic construction company. They had certain values. The local workers, labourers had a work culture, they were accommodative and very trustworthy.' Some four years later, he started his own construction company.

Faiz pointed down an alley to a dark grey house built in the dead end. 'I built that. Can you imagine constructing in this area? It was impossible to bring the lorries in. They parked on a wider road and the materials were carried in by men.' It being his old neighbourhood, people in the vicinity cooperated with the inconveniences caused, but it was not something he could take for granted.

One night, he drove away in his car when he realized he had a puncture. He changed his tyre only to discover another tyre was flat; the two had been deliberately punctured. It was a message – not to park where he had without permission. 'I reached home at midnight!'

We were now walking on the outer, slightly wider road.

'Everything is just the same, nothing has changed!' exclaimed Faiz, as we passed the Corporation dispensary, a dilapidated one-storey building. It was not something to celebrate. North Madras is known to have lagged far behind in development, and this was testimony to that lack of economic stimulus.

'For twenty years, they have marked this road for widening! It leads to Ennore, to the port there, and further north. Cycles, lorries, bullock cart, buses, cars everyone has to find their way on this road. It is really tough to drive in the traffic.'

In the sunny open air marketplace, bright red roses were being strung into long garlands. In the rows of small stalls, pulses and powdered spices lay heaped in basins, 'fancy' items such ribbons and bangles in others. Passing mounds of fresh vegetables, ripe bananas, large pomegranates and waxy apples, my eye chanced upon my favourite – custard apples. Big and green, just bordering on ripeness, I *had* to buy some to take home. It was the season; soon they would be gone.

I was immersed in choosing the best fruit the woman had on display, assessing their firmness by touch. When I had exhausted hers, I turned to the next stall which had even better fruit. Only someone had beat me to it. By the time he selected his lot, there weren't too many left. Still, I was content.

I followed Faiz as he negotiated his way across scraps of organic matter and garbage on the road. Vendors called out to me; clearly something in my appearance or perhaps the awkward time of day gave away the fact that I was new to the place.

One stall was devoted to lemons, arranged by size in flat baskets. The largest ones were spotless and fresh and a lovely yellow, almost the size of guavas. These were seasonal too. I hesitated, dying to buy some to turn into pickle. Only, what would Faiz think of me? Already he was lugging some of my custard apples! The salty-sweet tang of my imaginary lemon pickle evaporated from my tongue.

The meat shops lay further down the road. We came to a shop filled with old cycles. I thought, mistakenly, that it was a repair shop. Faiz paused in front of it. 'This shop has been here for ages.' Nostalgia seeped into his voice. 'I used to rent a cycle for 8 annas an hour.' When he enquired, we learnt that it still rented cycles, the price now Rs 8 an hour.

Ahead, a blue Metrowater tanker, water leaking out of its belly, sloshed to a halt near a bay stacked with empty buckets and narrow-necked pots or *kodams*. Made of translucent plastic, the pots radiated rainbow colours in the sun. People elbowed each other to get to the single pipe at the back that would give them water for the day. Curses thickened the air.

As we drove away, taking the arterial Thiruvottiyur High Road that was surprisingly narrow given that it enabled container-loaded heavy vehicles to access the industrial area further north of the city, Faiz was lost in thought.

'Thank God my parents moved from here, so my perceptions widened. Otherwise, I would have had only one idea of what Islam is about.' Decrepit buildings, broken culverts, loads of rubble, we drove several kilometres before I saw greenery. Passing Robinson Park now named Arignar Anna Poonga where at a seminal meeting in 1949 the DMK party was born, RSRM Lying-In Hospital – the result of a wealthy man's largesse, down pot-holed roads, we swung onto a clean stretch of Royapuram from where the harbour was visible. Huge cranes swam into view. Below, colourful containers were lined up like children's blocks. The sea was a suggestion of blue. Gazing out of the window, Faiz finished his line of thought: 'Having moved into the larger city, my horizon became larger.

'My father bought a small plot in Balaji Nagar. I designed and constructed our home there. It is in Royapettah near Triplicane. I like the atmosphere … it is a hub of activity. A lot of Muslims stay there, as also orthodox Brahmins and they peacefully coexist.'

Soon we were on North Beach Road, and arrived at territory that was recognizably Madras, with broader roads, large multi-storeyed buildings, the Indo-Saracenic main branch of the State Bank of India and then that famous landmark, Dare House at Parry's Corner.

Of the successive grants of villages by the Nawabs of the Carnatic to the British, most were to the north and north-west of the Fort. 'It is strange how north Madras did not grow after a point,' mused Faiz. 'Originally, this was the area where the city spread.' And we were doing a reverse journey, homing past Burma Bazaar, the sprawling High Court compound, the Reserve Bank, the dockyard to our left, to Fort St. George itself.

Faiz was currently working on a site in Pallikaranai to the far south-west where scores of dizzying, by Madras standards, high-rises had come up. Gated communities, swimming pools, club houses, schools, stores, these were just some of the amenities on offer.

In the past several years, the increase in construction, both private and by the state had resulted in a demand for semi-skilled labourers. Migrants from Bihar, Orissa and Bengal filled that gap, not just in construction but other areas as well such as security. Youngsters from the north-east, mainly Manipur, were increasingly visible behind the counters of many a store. In a city that had undergone an Anti-Hindi agitation, their presence and language stood out at once.

In terms of payment, a mason in Bihar might earn only about Rs 150 to Rs 200 a day, in a region where there was hardly any work to be had, and might even be cheated of that money by the contractor, whereas in Chennai he was assured a daily wage of Rs 550. 'So they migrate to the south where there is infrastructure work going on. It is big money for them. A male unskilled helper will get Rs 300, a female Rs 250.'

Faiz himself dealt with a sub-contractor, usually a Tamilian who provided the different specialized labour required. 'The local people have not objected to migrant workers coming here. They accommodate people from everywhere and are true Indians in that sense. The government used them as well when the new Assembly was built.'

In his own business, he had recently hired some masons from Kolkata. 'I asked one of them his name. "Mintu," he replied.' There was nothing in his appearance that gave Faiz a clue as to his background. "Mintu what?" I asked him. "Sheikh." It was only then that I knew he was a Muslim. So far they have worked hard. They come on time. Do not waste time. They go on working until the light fades. They do not watch the clock. They live on the site. The contractor allocates a place for them, gives them provisions and firewood to cook with. They are his responsibility.'

However the main change in the city that worried Faiz, and led him to start the *Islamic Forum for the Promotion of Moderate Thought*, was the growing intolerance on one side – 'In areas where growth is stagnant and there are few job opportunities, a lot of Muslims are being enticed by some televangelists to embrace radical ideologies' and the hardening of positions on the other – 'As a reaction to what people are reading in the news and seeing on the channels, they are forming an opinion that Muslims are not good people. They avoid having Muslim tenants or selling them an apartment in complexes. By building a 100-apartment complex for one community you are negating the idea of India, striking at the root of India's constitution – *All Indians are my brothers and sisters.*'

The way it was done was by using the excuse of food habits, not religion. 'A nice way of excluding Muslims is by saying "We do not want anybody who eats non-vegetarian." Now many Muslims are vegetarians … but they will not get a place to stay. This attitude has to change.'

That said, 'I love this city, and cannot imagine myself living in another city.' And in order of geographical preference, Faiz echoed the experience of many others in the city in saying, 'I am lucky I live in India and in India, in Tamil Nadu. It is a wonderful state. The most peaceful state in India. I am proud to be Tamilian.'

12

Wired and Wireless

'I saw the true effect of blogging during the tsunami.'
Kiruba Shankar

Technology has not only created a new space in the city, that of cyberspace, but also rearranged hierarchies and traditional modes of contact. The spread of the mobile phone means that electricians and carpenters and plumbers can be summoned in an emergency without having to send someone to fetch them. My dhobi invariably ends up calling to remind me that I have to collect my ironed clothes. Priests insouciantly check their messages even while declaiming verses in front of a *homa* fire.

The internet offers a neutral and open space for women to express themselves. Those at the receiving end of domestic violence especially, find the information they need under the cloak of anonymity. A lot of women who would hesitate to visit a counselling centre can reach out for help through the net.

The city has adopted technology-led change in a big way. Recently the story of an imaginative auto driver who provides free Wi-Fi, a tablet to access the net, magazines, newspapers and a mobile charging service to his customers went viral on the net. Even in the area of music and dance – bastions of tradition, one would think – technology is put to use in innovative ways. Teachers interact with students across the globe via Skype. Artistes have found a free means of publicity in Facebook and of course YouTube allows entire concerts to be shared, if that hasn't already been done via live streaming.

To try and understand the impact of this embrace of technology, I approached Kiruba Shankar, one of the earliest bloggers in the city.

At a time in the mid-nineties when few homes in India had a computer, and even fewer had a dial-up connection, Kiruba Shankar was among the first to harness the far-reaching power of the internet.

From maintaining a blog, to gathering fellow 'bloggers' at a camp in Chennai, to using various social media sites as they were invented – personal website, Wikipedia, Ryze, LinkedIn, Orkut, YouTube, Podcasting, Facebook, Twitter, Flickr, to name just a few – Kiruba has explored them all, while also keeping pace with changes in technology.

Well before I met him at his home in Virugambakkam – a congested downscale locality on the north-western out-skirts now amalgamated into the city – I was acquainted with his cheerful wife and parents, two bright little daughters, and obtained directions to reach his home, through his blog. I also knew that he changed his look every year, and could expect to find good-looking Kiruba with a beard, sans ponytail, sans handlebar moustache. And now seated in the small hall of his '2 BHK', his website visible on the laptop placed between us, I found him confident and extremely articulate.

'It all began when my articles were not accepted for publication by mainstream magazines, even though I was the editor of my college magazine. I hated to see them going waste.' Where others might have been discouraged, seeing in the rejection a comment on the quality of their writing, Kiruba was unfazed. 'Companies were offering free hosting.

So, instead of shoving it in my desk drawer, I stored it on the net.'

The result was gratifying. 'I had readers from all over the world ... more readers than the print run of those magazines! This was before the word blog came into being. I'm sure all those readers stumbled on my articles through search engines. It was very heartening. I understood the power of the internet. The power of being read, being appreciated, being discovered, it was a big thrill.'

Kiruba was captivated by that subversive quality of the net which allowed him to circumvent traditional power structures and to spread his reach beyond man-made boundaries. It opened up new spaces for him, encounters with people he would otherwise have never met. It also demonstrated the sort of social mobility that his family had sought for him when they sent him to boarding school near Madras.

'I was born and brought up in a small little picture-postcard village called Sooramangalam near Pondicherry. It was on the border of Tamil Nadu and Pondicherry, so there were many houses where one half fell in Tamil Nadu and other in Pondicherry. These houses would have two electricity meters!' exclaimed Kiruba.

While his father and grandfather were traditionally involved in agriculture and farming, Kiruba was more a passive observer when young. 'On my paternal side, we grew sugarcane. My mother's side grew a variety of crops ... paddy, tomatoes, brinjals.'

Kiruba's grandmother was literate, unusual for her time and circumstances. 'In the village, whether you had the means or not, everyone aspired to an "English-medium" education for their children and if this was in a convent school, even better.' So Kiruba Shankar was sent some 200 km away to boarding school in Chengalpattu near Madras.

'I think the mix of the modern and the traditional in me stemmed from there. I had the ability to traverse city life but was also taught to have respect for agriculture, land. Even now, when you step on land, you do not wear shoes, out of respect for *bhoomi*, Earth. I don't always follow that … when it is ploughed and turns hard, I don't. But the sentimental respect is always there.'

Kiruba was the only son, more importantly, the only child. His parents began to miss him, so when complications arose with their land, they sold part of it and moved to Madras enrolling him in a day-school there. 'Slowly many of our people stopped doing agriculture, moved away from the village to the city for education. Also, agriculture, for all that hard work, wasn't as remunerative as earlier. The cost of labour kept going up.'

But soon enough it was time for Kiruba to leave them and head off to college in Tumkur, Karnataka to study Instrumentation Engineering. 'It was a dry subject and I had no idea why I was studying this but the campus was a mini India and I loved meeting people from different states. Great exposure, for a guy like me from a village.'

It was in college that Kiruba first used e-mail. 'Internet came to India in 1995. BSNL provided dial-up lines. From Tumkur I had to take a bus to Bangalore. There, travelling to the Indian Institute of Science, making my way inside to the IT department, I would get to send e-mail! Compared to post, in the blink of an eye it travelled thousands of miles – it really caught my fancy.' Not everyone had access to the internet and the very fact of having sent an e-mail ensured that Kiruba re-entered campus a hero.

On graduation, Kiruba joined a business which also had a net café in Chennai – 'Who in their right mind after finishing a BE will go work in a browsing centre? It was wonderful …

I got time to sit and use the internet.' He also began to write for *DQ* magazine. 'Because of my interest in writing and IT, I got a job in Satyam Infoway. We still joke that the office, the entire second floor of Tidel park, was Asia's largest browsing centre.'

His parents and he had moved far inland to Virugambakkam. At the same time, there was an abiding sense of loss. 'In the village, it signals distress to sell land, like a death. Not actively doing agriculture is very sad, for an agricultural family. It was like killing the root.'

Alongside, Kiruba had started blogging, maintaining a sort of online diary, and this foray into unknown territory was to bring him fame. 'Maybe it was the time, the early part of the net, 1998 or '99, there were so few of us, maybe just five or six in Madras, that people were just appreciative of the material online.' In fact, Kiruba believes that 'Chennai was one of the earliest absorbers of technology. At one time, we had the largest number of blog meets and Twitter meets. Later, Anna University', a renowned institution with over 250 engineering colleges under its umbrella, 'was one of the first Universities to have blogging/social media as part of the curriculum in 2000.'

He discovered that he enjoyed sharing his experiences online, talking about issues that related to his life. Similarly, he was attracted to blogs written with a degree of honesty which involved him in the journey of the blogger's life. 'Each time I use an anecdote to illustrate a point, people love it. The people who read my blog, follow me on Facebook, and have become my friends. So the blog is a long story of my life. It morphed as the platforms changed, but what has *not* changed is the facility to tell my story online.'

And what was it about his story that interested people? What was the Kiruba magic, I asked him.

Kiruba has no pretensions; his answer was straightforward. 'They like to see a fairly unknown, lower middle class, ordinary guy just like them. They think of me as a guy who follows his heart and does what he does and tells the world about his experiences ... good and bad. People love storytelling, experiences.'

To help me understand better, Kiruba drew out a brown manila envelope from his papers. 'It is a contract from Jaico publishers. I just signed the contract, with a heavy heart and I will tell my readers why – because the contract is tilted very favourably towards the publisher! I will post a photo of this envelope and the contract and voice my feelings. When my book on media marketing comes out, they will be able to visualize the journey from contract to publication. They like the journey and they are being educated on the process, what happens behind the scenes.'

Listening to him, I got the sense that each post he shared memorializing his life helped his followers navigate social situations and experiences that their background might not have equipped them for. Kiruba's blog ensured democratizing of experiences; if he could coast through them, then potentially so could any reader of the blog irrespective of her social class or lack of savoir faire.

I am a lurker, very happy to surf and read endlessly but would shrink from presenting myself day in and day out on a blog. Paradoxically, Kiruba's story interested me because of his enthusiastic use of new platforms on the internet, his insouciant ability to breach the boundaries between private and public life online. I was curious about the sort of personality that would be comfortable revealing private details about himself – home, wife, children, interests, broadcasting them to the vast anonymity of the internet. Worse, from my point of view, someone comfortable with hosting complete strangers at his home via the Couchsurfing network. Did he not feel *exposed*, open to danger and risk?

Puzzled that anyone could see the internet in that way, Kiruba considered the idea. 'I am passionate about meeting new people. It is a way to meet people, put a face to the name. I have had some wonderful experiences across the world, been hosted for free by some great people thanks to Couchsurfing.'

When he hosts people in turn, 'I take all the couch surfers to Koyambedu market for the sheer buzz and zest for life one finds there! It's nearby, shall we go and take a look?'

I had never been to Koyambedu, so I jumped at the opportunity though Kiruba warned me, 'It is one of the dirtiest places in Chennai.'

Soon we were at the sprawling complex, heading to the flower section. Urine, fresh shit, puris being fried, Lifebuoy soap, rotting vegetable matter, sewage, it was an olfactory assault. I gave up trying to hold my breath.

'This is the real Chennai, Asia's largest vegetable market,' said Kiruba. 'I love the visual impact of all that colour, the aroma in the flower section. And then the miles of vegetables, so fresh. Watching people bargain, I can do that for hours.'

Inside the enormous concrete structure, a maze almost, we passed fresh garlands being woven, baskets of white lotus and pink lilies, and stacks of betel leaves. To get to the flowers, we tramped over sodden discarded stems, slippery bark, old flowers. The stalls were stark, plain enclosures lit with a dangling lamp, empty of everything except heaps of flowers in the centre. Each stall displayed a particular variety. Jasmines, tuberoses, marigolds, roses. Roses were not just roses, but genetically advanced 'star' roses, old-fashioned '*panneer*' roses … red, pink, yellow, multi-colour. One had to know what one wanted.

'It can be an overwhelming experience for someone on their first visit to India,' I said, responding to Kiruba's remark about couch surfers.

'Certainly! But some of them want to know why it is not in the guide books! They love it.'

His enthusiasm notwithstanding, some of those couch-surfing experiences could not have been entirely pleasant; one can only assess another human being in person.

'It's like a buffet,' conceded Kiruba. 'The set of people we meet, some people you like, some you don't, it is the same case with online. Even though you meet hundreds of people you choose whom you want to keep in touch with. There will be negative-minded people who want to attack you, don't like you, will be jealous, want to mar your reputation, but equally I have made great friends who share similar interests,' he explained patiently to me.

It is precisely this fearless embrace of faceless human beings across the globe that allowed Kiruba to be of help during the tsunami in 2005 that affected the lives of countless fisherfolk along the coastline of Tamil Nadu.

'I saw the true effect of blogging then. A few of us got into a car and drove on the East Coast Road. It was around afternoon. By then the relief work had started pouring in. To my shock we saw clothes strewn for kilometres and kilometres. Clothes unbundled, just flung by the side of the highway. When we enquired at the fishing hamlets, they said, "Everyone gives us only torn clothes, old dresses … all sorts of clothes. But we need other things – food and water." There was a big gap between what they needed and what they got. At the same time, people far away wanted to know how they could help. So I blogged that this is what they need: borewells and water, books for children to get back to school. The highest priority among the fishermen was nets because they had lost their boats and nets. It would help them get back on their feet. My blog post created an instant community of maybe 18,000 to 20,000 people, a tangible reaction.'

Kiruba learnt that while Tamils and non-Tamils alike wanted to donate money, they were sceptical about the government-run relief funds. 'They did not think the money they gave would actually reach the poor. I got requests asking me to show them the end result … where their money was being given. So we decided we would not be involved directly in accepting the money; rather we would act as facilitators, connecting the giver and receiver. We asked all our volunteers to document the actual handing over, say a kerosene stove donated to a family, with a photo or video. Faraway donors found that trustworthy.'

The most meaningful experience of all was at MGR Thittu, a small island away from the mainland, almost destroyed and with very few survivors left. 'It took fifteen minutes to cross the sea to reach them. They had no internet nor phones and were isolated. Mainly they needed nets, apart from basics. We made sure that the money reached the suppliers of nets, who then distributed it to them.'

It was the first time Kiruba saw the power of information being used in a practical way to help the poorest of poor. 'I found it was a beautiful win-win scenario. Matching needs with the donor's satisfaction. Importantly, I saw some of the most honest government officials working to help the homeless there. They thanked us too!'

While Kiruba talked, I shopped happily for flowers, as we meandered past the stalls. Because it was a wholesale market, prices here were one tenth of what I would pay in my neighbourhood. By now I had a bag of about fifty roses, red and yellow, for Rs 20. Four lotus for Rs 10, ten fuschia gerberas for Rs 20 and lovely dahlias at five for Rs 10. I eyed a bunch of delicate orchids but they seemed relatively expensive at Rs 100.

'Let's walk to the fruit section,' suggested Kiruba.

Transformed by the tsunami experience, in 2007, Kiruba took the life-changing decision 'wish I had done it ten years earlier' to quit his 'constricting' nine-to-five job with Sulekha.com and work at building the online presence of various companies, also undertaking website design, while offering his expertise as a social media/digital marketing consultant and motivational speaker at large.

Here too he discovered that 'all these social media platforms were supremely helpful in opening up professional avenues. The last few jobs I got, I was never interviewed. It was as though my online self, my podcasts, blog, would go ahead of my physical self, would convince on my behalf and the only conversation with prospective clients was their wanting to know when I could join.'

Some would argue that it is a self-fulfilling endeavour; the more Kiruba projects the image of being a tech-savvy expert, the more opportunities he gets to build that expertise.

Kiruba continued animatedly, 'Social media is a powerful image-building tool. It is a great way to build a brand around yourself. In India very few people build their own brand ... because of our very Indian quality of being *modest*. Do not talk only about yourself, you should not boast. We have this voice of the elders in our head. I consciously did that, built my brand, not as a way to hype things up but to talk about what is *me*. To say: *I am not perfect but in my all imperfectness this is me.*'

If there is one virtue deeply ingrained in the city's culture, it is modesty: no flamboyant display of wealth and never 'blowing', to translate the Tamil word, one's trumpet. Kiruba would locate a shift in the city in its changing notions of 'modesty'. 'A very visible and tangible change from Madras to Chennai is that while earlier we felt awkward about saying good things about ourselves now it has reached a stage where people are throwing parties so that they will have photos to post on Facebook. People are less conscious talking about themselves. When you get sixty likes and forty comments, the instant recognition is addictive. And so we tend to live two lives, who we are and who we aspire to be. The online world gives us the opportunity to portray ourselves in a certain way. In that sense our online self is always better than the offline self. We all choose the best photo to post.'

It was not yet noon, but the fruit market was hot. Fans whirred ineffectually and I began to feel sorry for the men who spent most of their day here in the stultifying building. And their day began very early, at around 2 or 3 a.m. when the fresh produce came in lorries from all around the state and other cities such as Bangalore.

It was Kiruba's turn to buy, and he loaded up on fruits. Oranges, chikoos and apples. 'For today's lunch,' said Kiruba, picking the best of bright red pomegranates.

How far has technology helped enforce change in the city, I asked Kiruba. He replied, 'We are wonderful armchair activists. We are not comfortable carrying a placard, the way you see people do in Delhi or northern cities. In the south, if we want to convey our concern, we want to do it in the relative comfort of our home, through Facebook. Take the Anna Centenary Library campaign,' in 2011, when the city collectively felt a sense of outrage that the popular Rs 172 crore state library was to be converted into a paediatric hospital. 'There was a call out: Let us all meet and occupy the library movement. Whereas the Facebook page had two lakh likes on it, only a few hundred actually showed up at the given time.'

His own boss now, and enjoying thoroughly the freedom to structure his time, Kiruba discovered online 'niche communities that you will not find in the mainstream space. I collect record players and records. When I created a website and put up my collection, the number of people who wrote to me … it was amazing. A simple interest of mine opened up to introduce me to others who had this interest.'

Similarly with comic books. 'I am very passionate about comics, want to collect as many as I can for me, my kids and the children in my apartment complex. I got a call from a person in Chennai, he said, "I have been collecting Tarzan from the sixties. Clippings worth lakhs for a collector. I have everything in a box, just come and take it." He said the reason he was giving it to me was that he could see from my site that I was genuinely passionate about comics.

'Visitors from elsewhere, they always say Chennai is a boring place. But there are such interesting communities here! Cycling, ultimate frisbee, *silambam*, juggling … to name just a few, that is awesome.'

Even with cycling as a sport, changing times are evident. 'In Madras, the cycle was seen as transportation, looked down upon and associated with the poor. In Chennai, cycling is now an elite sport activity.'

Energized by the interest his followers take in his adventures, 'they like what you give and they respond. They respond so you are willing to give them more of what they like'. Kiruba participated in the Tour of Tamil Nadu, a mini Tour de France, on a sleek Schwinn Searcher that cost him Rs 18,000.

'Cycling 900 kms in seven days! I doubt I would I have done it on my own, torturing myself over all that distance, if not for the publicity and blog. I did it because I had a platform to share my experiences. It motivates me to do new things every year.'

Kiruba paused, his attention drawn to the ripe pineapple in his hand. 'Imagine if this is selling for Rs 20 here, what the poor farmer would have got for it.' As we headed back to his home, he shook his head sorrowfully. 'The more I think about it, a farmer can just about break even. The middlemen make the most profit.'

Post-lunch, enjoying the burst of flavour from mouthfuls of glossy red pomegranate seeds, it seemed to me that by opening himself to all that the internet could offer, Kiruba had made Chennai, and specifically his home, the centre of the universe. Experience and interaction both stemmed from *and* radiated inwards from all over the world to this single human being located in an otherwise standard maze of apartments in an unremarkable part of the city.

With time, his part of the city has changed. 'Metamorphosis! When we came here it was a suburb, outside Chennai and not a cool place to live in. Ten years ago, we had to go to T Nagar to buy anything. Now everything is here, malls, restaurants, even Satyam theatre!'

Elsewhere, 'I love Mylapore, the mada streets around the temple. I love that in the early mornings, around 4 a.m. it is almost as though time stood still. It is so unhurried. People wake up to go and buy milk. At that quiet time before the traffic crowds the roads, it is possible to go back to Madras, the way it used to be.'

For all his outward success, the sense of being landless haunted him. 'It hurt me. I wanted to go back to my roots, rewind the clock, return to my glory days. Visiting Sooramangalam I would hear the villagers say, "Such a great family, all this was your land." That my forefathers did all that, but the generations could not maintain it, I felt bad.' He feared that his two bright city-bred daughters would think milk came out of Aavin packets rather than a cow's udder.

And so, Kiruba acquired 9 acres of farm land in Rettanai village near Tindivanam, some 133 kilometres away. On the weekends he spends time with his family at Vaksana Farms, unwired from the digital world. 'I told myself it is a journey, even if I did not make money or made losses, I would be okay with that. Farming on weekends recharges me tremendously to come back to the city and live my Monday to Friday life.'

He understood soon enough that it was the 'joy of unplugging', not being connected 24/7 that made the farming experience wonderful. His eyes lit up as he said, 'I want to recreate a *nandanavanam*, a fruit orchard. You should be able to pluck the fruit you want yourself, that's my dream.'

At the farm, Kiruba came up against ancient notions of what a landowner must and must not do. 'I enjoy wearing a dhoti, folded up around my thighs like any labourer, and mucking around with the wet earth. But you quickly lose respect among the villagers when you try to do it. If I wore a white shirt and had a man hold an umbrella over my head, if I played the '*Mudalali*' and hurled the choicest of abuses at them, I would get the work done faster!'

Still, Kiruba attempted hard physical labour. 'In the beginning, I was physically incapable of doing it, my body was not used to working two hours in the blazing sun.' Different rhythms were at play here, the cycle of seasons, the complete submission to nature. A seedling would come to fruition in its own time, there was no rushing it. 'Only when you do the hard labour, do you appreciate the fruit. When a vegetable grows on its stalk, the way you treat is vastly different from the indifference with which you buy it in the city.

'I intend to marry traditional farming with modern technology. If I can mix them in the right proportion then nothing like that. I see disturbing trends in the village. Take casuarina … A farmer lovingly grows it for three years. He then makes x rupees, but the agent makes the same amount in one day! Unacceptable! Through technology and the power of information, I want to cut the middleman out.'

He now hosts WWOOFers (World Wide Opportunities in Organic Farms), people who are passionate about farming from around the world at his farm. 'Come one weekend,' he invited me, persuasively.

I am yet to take up his offer. You see, vicariously, online I have participated in the bhoomi puja propitiating the gods and planets, watched his self-designed red-tiled home rise out of flat earth, dug furrows with a plough, admired the different kinds of mud huts in the area, felt distraught at the way beautiful cranes are poisoned by villagers and sympathized with Kiruba when he incurred a loss on his recent harvest of millets.

The boy who came to the city to study and earn a living as an adult leaves it every weekend to water the earth, transplant paddy. Entrepreneur, author, speaker, podcaster, people connecter; his weblog now has another word describing himself: farmer.

Afterword

In the streets, the neighbourhood, one not only sees what exists but also remembers what no longer does. It is this thread of memory that provides continuity; though one may walk the same street everyday it is always changing and always the same.

And so, south of the Adyar river, in Shastri Nagar, as I stroll down the main avenue that was once simply 2nd Avenue, but is now MG Road, I think of the time in the seventies, when the area south of Adyar was still developing. It meant there were few concrete structures, whether houses or shops, and lots of empty land. Today, this avenue has been transformed with big shops, bright signage flashing brand names, and lots of traffic. Still a residential area, many of the apartments have shops on their ground floor, shut off from the road by air-conditioning.

I start at one end, heading towards the Velankanni church and Elliot's beach. There is an old woman selling clay lamps, off the footpath. Earthen pots, pans, lids, piggy-banks, all of these occupy her open air 'shop' apart from the diya-lamps in different sizes.

As is anywhere in the world, it is the human interactions that define one's experience of a place. One Deepavali, I had stopped to buy lamps from her. All around us the noise of firecrackers, bomb after bomb exploding, rose into the sky. The metallic smell of flash gunpowder was in the air, as also the palpable quickening of approaching festivity.

I bought twenty-four and offered her a currency note. It was far larger than her bill. She did not have change. Noticing the torn sleeve of her blouse, her faded tattered sari, her world-worn wrinkled skin, I told her to keep the change. Swiftly she bent down, picked up a few small clay toys – miniature cooking utensils – and beaming, gave them to me.

It is a lesson I have not forgotten. The clay toys are placed near my favourite books in my room. I look at them everyday.

I soon reached a building that came up more than thirty years ago; a set of five shops. In one of them, two young men had set up a Rupa lending library, and soon a pharmacy and a bakery had appeared too. Every evening I would set off on my new bicycle, both to find new books to read and chat with the owners, thrilled as only a twelve-year-old could be that these grown-up boys actually talked to me. The paint was fresh, the books were new, the wooden counters new too but our custom alone did not provide them enough of a profit. To my dismay, in a year or so, they shut shop. Nataraja Medicals and Venson's Bakery are still going strong.

Decades later, I discovered those counters, distinctive, white with a pink wooden flower, in a 'fancy' store about a kilometre away, and it is this sort of arcane knowledge that everyone possesses about their own neighbourhood.

When Rupa closed, my mother, who has a voracious appetite for books matched by the ability to read them extremely fast, and I had to venture further in search of books. In Adyar, we found a dimly lit one set in the nook of a dingy building, which had books uniformly bound and stamped with its name. The covers were scuffed and the pages yellowing, but that did not deter us. Books! Reading material! Boredom abated! One had to choose from what was available, and if I am up on my PG Wodehouse and Perry Mason, Mills & Boon, Edgar Wallace and Agatha Christie mysteries, it is thanks to this library. Sadly, smaller libraries such as these have vanished.

Walking on, there are many things that feed my senses. *Swara*-notes from a violin caressed by a lover's bow; the sight of plump jasmines strung for a newly-wed to gift his bride; *maghrib* prayer suffusing the air; a pyramid of tender coconuts and the flash of a rusted blade hacking one open – the eternal anticipation of just how sweet its water might be, how delicate the white membrane inside; the dazzle of orange Kanjeevaram silk; devotional music blaring from a popular shrine; a spread of rotting garbage; wet bunches of edible leaves; the stink of freshly caught *vanjaram* fish; watermelons sliced pink; the joy of pinching a baby's cheek.

At a cycle repair shop, there is a young labourer getting air filled in the tyres of his new cycle. Tasselled leather sheath on the metal bar between the seat and handle-bar; steel peacock and a spear atop tall spikes on either side of the front wheel, in allegiance to the handsome god Muruga; a shining steel box with a lock and a polished carrier at the back; spokes clamped with colourful plastic trinkets – these are the accessorized wheels of a proud bachelor!

I have reached Vannandurai, which as its name suggests, is an area inhabited by dhobis. In the less sophisticated seventies, there were a cluster of unpretentious shops, no different than those in a village. And the short walk from home seemed like an expedition to procure supplies. A shop that sold raw groundnuts, horsegram, puffed and flattened rice heaped them in enormous cane baskets that were both display and stock. The essential 'tea-*kadai*' – a stall selling hot tea and butter-biscuits – was a shack made of dried coconut fronds, lit by a kerosene lantern at night. I was fascinated by the long rope that dangled near bunches of semi-ripe bananas, smouldering at one end. Periodically, men would catch hold of it to light their beedis. An improvement on this was a lamp with a glass chimney, and slivers of paper in a tin next to it.

Several mills operated to grind wheat, turmeric, chillies, even soapnut and *shikakai* for the hair. One could never be sure, despite the operator vigorously shaking the cloth funnel, that the quantity one brought back was roughly the same as the grain poured into the mill.

Reputed companies began to offer ground and packaged spices and cereals, and the mills vanished, as did the shop with its ware heaped in baskets. But the coffee mills remain, for freshly ground coffee is always in demand. Tea shops now are more organized, operating from a proper building with electricity and a name board.

The chatter of typewriters rang out from 'institutes' for stenographers, at least two to a neighbourhood. You could learn typing and shorthand, pass an exam and fully empowered by a knowledge of squiggles, hope to get a job. They have been replaced by net cafes, those same not too clean rooms in a bazaar now packed with dated monitors and sticky keyboards.

When the first department stores came to the area, people flocked to them, enjoying the sight of shelves lined with a great range of things. Then newer stores cropped up in the nineties offering the pleasures of self-service, and it seemed that the proprietors of the smaller grocery stores would not be able to compete. But they did, perhaps in large measure because we liked the personal touch of the owner, his greeting, his ready willingness to sell a quantity even as small as 50 grams. There was a different kind of charm here, watching a kilo of rice being weighed and twine wound around the heavy paper cone it was packed in, scanning the garlanded photograph high on the wall, that of a father or grandfather who had set up the shop. But recently two such stores that had held out for long have closed, and each time I pass the premises, I cannot but remember the faces of those store owners, and that of their ancestors.

Perhaps the most surprising change was the embrace of ready made idli batter. The taste of idli and dosai varied across homes depending on their secret ratio of rice to lentils, how long they fermented the dough and whether or not they slipped in some fenugreek seeds. Somewhere around the mid-nineties, it became possible to distribute batter in plastic packets that were stored in coolers across shops. Homes that had bought heavy-duty batter grinding machines jettisoned them without a thought. One friend told me she was able to make the thinnest of dosais thanks to its 'fine' quality, something that endeared her to her demanding husband. The other day, I was amazed to see a new sort of enterprise, a shop that sells only freshly ground idli batter.

At the turn of the century, youngsters barely out of college earned handsome salaries at BPOs. Cafes, food courts, Wi-Fi enabled hangout joints – the city catered to them. Pizza restaurants sprung up by the dozens and the concept of 'unlimited refills' overturned the long prized virtue of 'waste-not'. I once saw a table littered with half-empty Coke glasses at a popular pizza place; a sign of changed times.

Around the time when sleek models from Hyundai, Honda and Ford on the road began to outnumber and outpace the slow Ambassador and the even slower Premier Padmini or Herald, the police got a makeover as well. All of a sudden, men and women in smart khaki uniforms were visible in Hyundai Accents with sirens and light-racks with red and blue beacons. So posh are the patrol cars, we are still getting used to the idea.

Past the shop where an evil hunch-backed tailor ruined my expensive silk blouse, past the one which stores delicious granular ghee from Utthukuli, past the Chinese hairdressers', past a gypsy selling colourful bead necklaces, past the vessel shop where you can still get your initials etched on stainless steel dishes.

A straggle of people at the bus stop wait patiently for an iconic 23A or 29C or 47A or 23C that will take them hurtling across the city. My own favourite is 21D which affords a view of the entire Marina from a height. We now have air-conditioned buses, very Chennai, but I am yet to try them.

Ahead, the avenue widens, lined with raintrees, the copper pod, fragrant tree jasmine or *panneer poo*, gulmohar and the ever present neem. But today, the *konrai* is in bloom, and the boring green of other trees is no match for a yellow so glorious that it adorns Shiva's matted hair.

To walk is to measure the city with one's own body, pace and breath competing with each other. Treading ground, there is a primal link between oneself and one's surroundings – the heat, the rain, the humidity. At the Annai Velankanni church, I am reminded of the thousands who throng this road during the annual festival in September, some making a pilgrimage on foot from remote areas.

Turning left – strong winds, Elliot's beach aka 'Bessie', and the restless blue of the Bay of Bengal.

I have always lived close to the sea, and like many others, I take the endless blue and wide beaches completely for granted, not heading to nearby Bessie for days, but when I do, I always accept the embrace of its salt-laden breeze with pleasure.

It is in the evenings that the beach is most crowded, when people stream out of their confining homes. Retired men in a circle, sari-clad women in sneakers, excited families from the mofussil dressed in their best for an outing to the beach, children shooting at balloons, college students out and about, wand-bearing women telling fortunes and urchins selling the famous sundal and *murukku* in glass-fronted bins – by 5 p.m. the sands, otherwise a desert during the day, are gay with colour.

While the Marina affords a view of far-off ships anchored at the harbour, one mostly gets to see catamarans at Bessie. Fishing nets spread out to dry, wooden boats, fish frying in the makeshift stalls ... these are all reminders of the presence of fishermen in the nearby hamlet Urur Kuppam. They still rule the sea, this one expanse of the city that is theirs alone as it has been for centuries.

On 31 October 2012, as is usual for that time of the year, a cyclone was surging towards the coast. The sky was overcast, it was raining intermittently. Across the city, trees were falling, felled by the fierce winds. The beach was mostly empty; it was afternoon. In the grey mist of sky and cloud and rain-spray an apparition loomed just about a hundred metres away in the raging sea. It was surreal. Where there was always just water and sky, appeared the long black hull of an oil tanker, its upper half barely visible.

The Pratibha Cauvery had been adrift since morning. All its SOS signals had gone unanswered, cyclone Nilam was close to landfall, and now its keel had hit the sea-bed. The captain ordered the crew to abandon ship. It was not the best of decisions. The winds were tossing the tanker about as though it were a toy. The waves were monstrously tall, intent on swallowing the vessel. No sooner had the lifeboats been lowered into the sea than they capsized, dumping twenty-two men into the angry waters.

From the beach, a group of fishermen had seen the distress rockets fired from the ship. Now, two hours later, they could see some of the men struggling to hold onto the boats. It was clear that though some sailors were trying desperately to save their lives, they ought to have been swimming in the direction of the waves. Vadivelu, the strongest swimmer at Urur Kuppam jumped on to Gopi's boat with Kalaimani, Madhan and Udayamoorthy. They crossed the choppy sea to try and help the stranded men.

They saved sixteen lives that day. One of the crew died and another five were missing. The fishermen lost their own nets, catamaran and mechanized boat when cyclone Nilam did hit land. Days later, they were awarded Rs 1 lakh each by the state government.

In the week that followed, people thronged the shoreline to gawk at the stricken Pratibha Cauvery. On the face of it, there was nothing to see except a ship the length of 174 metres. There were no people on it, nor was it moving. Yet, excitement gripped everyone, and soon roads leading to the beach were jammed. It was a very Madras response.

And in that response was a clue to the city's nature. Here was spectacle, here was drama. Here was entertainment, free, U-rated. Something larger than our humdrum routine had arrived at our shores. It turned 'city'zens and the rural populace into child-like spectators alike, exclaiming in wonder at the unusual. Saluting the bravery of fishermen, usually neglected by all. And enjoying the chance to connect with the spirit of the seas, otherwise off-limits to most.

Not worth a single seed of mustard

…

If you weigh
worldly life
against the life of the spirit,
it is not worth a single seed of mustard.

…

— Vanmikiyar

Purananuru 358

Select Bibliography

The Madras Tercentenary Commemoration Volume, 1979.

Madras, Chennai: A 400-year Record of the First City of Modern India, edited by S Muthiah, Palaniappa Brothers, 2008.

Chennai Not Madras: Perspectives on the City, edited by AR Venkatachalapathy, Marg Publications, 2006.

Political History of Carnatic under the Nawabs, NS Ramaswami, Abhinav Publications, 1984.

Madras Discovered, S Muthiah, Affiliated East-West Press Pvt. Ltd, 1987.

The Grip of Change, P Sivakami, Orient BlackSwan Pvt Ltd, 2006.

Bird Life in A City, M Krishnan, The Illustrated Weekly of India, May 24,1953.

Love Stands Alone: Selections from Tamil Sangam Poetry, translated by ML Thangappa, edited by AR Venkatachalapathy, Viking, 2010.

The pages of 'Metroplus', *The Hindu*.

Adyar Times.

Acknowledgements

I thank all of the following who gave generously of their time while being interviewed, or helped the completion of this book in other ways.

Al-Hajj Nawab Ghulam Mohammed Abdul Ali, The Eighth Prince of Arcot, Dr Beatrix D'Souza, A Faizur Rahman, the family of Indumati and M Krishnan, Kiruba Shankar, V Ramnarayan, Sarathbabu Elumalai, Saravana Sakthivale, K Seshadri, P Sivakami, Dr Uma Ram, and finally actor Vikram.

PM Belliappa, Divya Kumar, Jyotirmaya Sharma, Maanas Udayakumar, Mini Krishnan, Prince Frederick, Reena and Pradeep Bhanotha, PK Sadasivan and Bala, Saugata Mukherjee, Sravanthi Challapalli, Dr Sumita Kale and Vincent D'Souza.

I am grateful to AV Ilango, whose work I admire greatly, for allowing me to use a painting from his Chennai Series for the cover of this book.

The Pan Macmillan team: Pranav Kumar Singh, Sushmita Chatterjee and Pooja Pande who took a great deal of care while working on the manuscript.

The two poems quoted are from *Love Stands Alone: Selections from Tamil Sangam Poetry*, translated by ML Thangappa, edited by AR Venkatachalapathy, Viking, 2010.